The
i'Mpossible
Project:
Volume I

Reengaging With Life,
Creating a New You

Josh Rivedal

50 Authors

Skookum Hill Publishing
CROTON ON HUDSON, NEW YORK

Skookum Hill Publishing
55a Truesdale Dr.
Croton on Hudson, NY 10520

Thematic Editor: Josh Rivedal
Copyeditor: Pamela Cangioli
Cover Design: Simplelight.com and Benlin Alexander
Book Layout: Josh Rivedal

Ordering Information:
Quantity sales. Special discounts are available on quantity purchases by corporations, associations, and others. For details, contact the "Special Sales Department" at the address above. Contact the author directly at http://www.iampossibleproject.com for special fund-raising opportunities for charitable organizations.

The i'Mpossible Project: Volume 1: Reengaging With Life, Creating a New You/ Josh Rivedal.
ISBN 978-0-9860964-7-1

Acknowledgments

First, I want to thank my wife Candace for her love and support. When finding true love becomes possible, it makes many of the impossibilities in life truly possible. I cannot express how grateful I am for the support of the folks listed below. Some of them have helped champion this book, but all of them have held, loved, defended, and comforted one or more of the fifty authors in this first edition of *The i'Mpossible Project*. And of course, to my forty-nine authors, I am inspired and moved by your bravery, your storytelling, and your determination to help others through the obstacles you have had to overcome. Thank you.
 - Josh

Andrea Tugander, Ann Hirschman Schremp, Audrey Burger, Bart Andrews, Beverly Matthews, Candace Yoder, Carol Graham, Christine Cales, Darren Huddleston, Deborah Richards, Deirdre Sinnott, Diane Hughes, Donald Simpson, Eastern Missouri Chapter of AFSP, Elizabeth Kirshner, Elizabeth Makulec, Emilie Bakal, Emily DeProw, Emily Morris, Erin Poniewaz, Gail Sells, Gary Sullivan, Gisela Chlanda, Heather Jenkins, Heidi Chernich, Holden Strait, Ilana Danneman, Jane Beller, Janice Sullivan, Jenna Burton, Jennifer Huffman, Jessica Hooks, Jo Sells, JoElla Beegle, Jonathon Hyde-Burton, Joseph Rogan, Joshua Donnelly, Joshua Satok, Joshua Schwartz, Joshua Strait, Joy Howell, Judith Johnson, Julie Shaffer, Kacie Sandlin, Karen Nestingen, Karen Strait, Karen Wagner, Kathryn Greene, Kelly Norris, Kevin Briggs, Kevin Hines, Kristen Oesch, Lana Phillips, Laura Matlock-Hill, Lenore Reback, Leslie Shasha, Linda Ankney, Linda Manning, Lynda Braun, Margaret Hines, Mark Burton, Mark Graham, Mary Look, Maynard Howell, McKenzie DeProw, Melanie Massey, Melinda Huddleston, Michael Mondschein, Mikayla Burton, Monica Reagan, Nathan Hyde-Burton, Onnalita Sutton, Patty Hill, Paul Spell, Paula Sterling, Pauline Venieris, Phyllis Blackwelder, Phyllis Kukin, Merrick Kukin, Rebecca Seitz, Richard Strait Sr., Robbie Carcoba, Rose Terry, Rosie De Sanctis, Scott Perkins, Sharon Carr, Shayna Strait, Stacy Simpson, Steven Herevia, Susan Knape, Terri Harris, Thomas Hooks, Toby Grossman, Travis Tamerius, Valerie Starshak, Venita Mitchell, Wilfredo Coriano, William Kukin

Table of Contents

i'Mpossible Lived Experience

With Suicide 129

i'

....

Inspiration for
The i'Mpossible Project

FOR YEARS I'VE BEEN TELLING my personal story via an autobiographical thirty-character, one-man play *Kicking My Blue Genes in the Butt* (yes, I get along with the rest of the cast just fine). I've toured internationally with my one-man show in theaters, high schools, universities, juvenile detention centers, and one unfortunate college biology lab. In my story, following my father's suicide in my early twenties, a lawsuit from my mother over my father's inheritance, and a break-up with my long-term girlfriend—all in the span of twenty months—I fell into isolation, silence, and melancholy that eventually had me hanging out of my fourth-floor bedroom window contemplating taking my life.

But I pulled myself back inside and got help—first from my mom and then through trusted friends and professional counseling, all because I took a risk and opened up about my pain.

Now, after each presentation I talk about my recovery process and how I found a way to reengage with life.

After nearly every show, incredible people—complete strangers who might feel voiceless or worthless or simply unheard—confide in me powerful, personal stories on how they've overcome tremendous odds in their lives. These stories not only changed my life for the better, but also the life of the storyteller.

At one point or another in our lives, I—along with millions of other storytellers—took a chance on myself and said "I am possible." But why do a book about people's stories?

Stories Provide a Template for Success

Whenever I'm feeling particularly uninspired or low, one of my favorite activities is to read the biography of someone famous and look for the part of their life story where they had struggled. I find that I learn a lot more from a person's low points—my own included—rather than a highlight reel of their greatest achievements.

I'm deeply curious about how people reengage with life after a difficult, traumatic, or tragic event. How did they get back on the horse? In what ways did they succeed? What did they do that was "unsuccessful?" (Quick tangent: the word "fail" should be replaced in the English language with "lesson I learned on my way to success." Booyah.)

"If that woman can overcome her paraplegia to become a famous painter by using her teeth, then holy cow, I can do just about anything!"

"That guy lost his wife and daughter in a car accident and fell into tremendous grief, but then rebounded, found love again, and became the Vice President of the United States. If he can keep fighting on then, oh snap, I can keep on fighting, too."

When people give of themselves through the telling of their stories it makes the seemingly impossible in our lives tangible and attainable.

Stories Break Down Stigma

The world becomes much smaller. "That black guy," "that lesbian-chick," "that snarky-writer-guy who talks about suicide prevention" they all now have a name. David. Jamie. Josh. Each of these people has wants and needs to live, to love, to survive and thrive... just like every other human being.

But why include these particular stories in the book? Some of the topics inside this book are not ones typically found in an inspirational-style book: murder, post-traumatic stress disorder, and a transgender recording artist. Each story displays its own beauty and with each, the author uncovers a piece of themselves, showing us a moment in their lives where they've overcome a tremendous obstacle, transformed, or changed for the better. By doing so, they allow us to peel back and examine a layer of our own soul.

STORIES ARE A DEMAND FOR OUR CIVIL RIGHTS.

Slow down, Rivedal. Don't get so preachy. It's only the second page of the book.

I know. I just get really excited about this idea.

Once stigma is broken down because of the courage of the "abnormal" person telling their story, they are now viewed as a human being. They now have a seat at the proverbial table of equality. Jim Crow is repealed. Women's suffrage is enacted. Mental health laws are passed that empower and aid people with illnesses rather than traumatizing or criminalizing them.

That's the kind of world that I want to live in. Bam.

A COUPLE OF THINGS TO NOTE

This book is not written entirely by polished authors—some are and some are not. (A few of the authors might want to kick me in the shins after reading that last sentence... but I'll take my chances). Each story is unique, powerful and inspirational; a love letter of sorts to you, the reader, on how they've dealt with tremendous hardship and found a way to reengage with life in the aftermath.

I've edited each of the stories to a certain extent—not to fit my writing style, but rather to make sure the story arc of each is crystal clear. I hope I've done you a service with this.

Each story is no more than one thousand words. Sometimes we get bogged down in unnecessary details not imperative to the heart of what the story is actually about. The word limit is to give the story arc a laser-like focus and is for the reader with a short attention span (like me).

How should you read this book? Some of these stories are lighter and some are pretty heavy—take your time with it. Read it out of order. Focus on one story a week, and savor the deeper meaning, figuring out how it speaks to you ... or not. Read it however you want. If one (or more) of the stories inspires you and you want to pass it along—go right ahead.

QUIT YOUR YAKKING, JOSH

I actually had ten more pages and a couple of haikus to share, but fine... without further ado, I present to you fifty fantastic authors and *The i'Mpossible Project: Volume 1—Reengaging With Life, Creating a New You.*

(Cue the thunderous applause)

i'

....

Foreword
Kevin Hines

I N 2013, JOSH RIVEDAL released *The Gospel According to Josh: A 28-Year Gentile Bar Mitzvah*—his first book of what will surely be many. Josh found his voice expressing his family's terrible loss from his father's suicide, his own internal mental struggles, his suicidal ideations, his family's woes, and how he put himself back together. Josh's *Gospel...* is based in part on his acclaimed Off-Broadway show, first produced in New York City, now entitled *Kicking My Blue Genes in the Butt*, a unique one-man show, in which he plays thirty characters, sings seven songs, and spans his lifetime. Yep, it's just Josh. The stories he shares throughout this one-man show, keynote address, and memoir are taken directly from the real characters woven throughout his life. The book and show have both had astounding success.

All of Josh's endeavors have been nothing less than intriguing, educational, and highly entertaining! This thirty-something comedic entrepreneur never ceases to amaze. He shows us that it does not matter what pains you have experienced due to your own mental, emotional, and physical health. No matter such difficulties, and despite struggles, you can find hope, move forward, and give back to your community. He planted the seeds in countless hearts and minds, empowering individuals to look within themselves. He wants those his story touches to be the catalyst in saving their own lives. With his frequent blogging, his educational performances, his current social media project, his company, forthcoming books, plays, seminars, and his workshops, Josh is not slowing down anytime soon. This is his sophomore book and it's aptly titled *i'Mpossible.* It is clear not much is impossible for Josh Rivedal and those who heed his inspirational message.

The i'Mpossible Project, Reengaging With Life, Creating A New You captures the true essence of storytelling. Inside this book are fifty stories from people who have reached the brink of the proverbial cliff. Many of these authors came to a juncture in their lives where they firmly believed it was, in some manner or another, the end of the road. Some even attempted to die by suicide, but survived. Others have lived through devastating trauma. But in the aftermath of harrowing odds, each author learned and continued to thrive.

These are stories of "lived experience," and each one is unique and compliments the next. Each of these true tales is incredible, with the potential to help shape the lives of so many people and possibly prevent others from reaching their own dead end. Today, everyone who is featured in *The i'Mpossible Project* is actively fighting day in and day out for their mental, and physical well-being, pushing toward hope, and working tirelessly on themselves so they can inspire others.

The i'Mpossible Project is dedicated to capturing life at its worst, at the middle of the road, and eventually, at its best. These stories share with countless people the idea that, "If I can do it … so can you!" Josh epitomizes this very notion. He is a sounding board for their woes and is often a giant shoulder to lean on for people living through the roughest of mental health and suicidal conditions. In a time when suicide, mental and behavioral health problems, and taboo physical health conditions are becoming more and more talked about, this project shines. It is giving the average Joe and Jane a platform to share their lives with others, as well as the opportunity to help hundreds, thousands, and even millions. Every author and story in the book finds a new and innovative way to relate to people from all walks of life.

When you read this amazing literary feat, you may just walk away with an uplifting feeling that changes your entire perspective on the world and the seven billion who reside within it. Your empathy may also be tested, and your view on the ones closest to you may even be enlightened. Now, as each writer shares their story with the world, they not only guide others to a more well-balanced life—they have discovered the catharsis that guides each of them to the hope that helps heal. This book is imperative to the aid of so many onto #TheWayForward, onto a future lived well.

- Kevin Hines

Storyteller

Founder, 17th & Montgomery Productions

Families

"*YOU CAN KISS YOUR FAMILY and friends good-bye and put miles between you, but at the same time you carry them with you in your heart, your mind, your stomach, because you do not just live in a world but a world lives in you.*"

  - Frederick Buechner

The Florida Triangle

Suzanne Bachner

I HAD TO TELL THEM. There was no getting around it. I had promised myself—and them—to keep them in the loop. Although we all lived in New York, we were meeting up in Palm Beach, Florida to visit a family friend. I sat on the edge of the bed with my husband, Bob, in my parents' hotel room. Mom and Dad sat in chairs across from us.

"Remember how I told you that I hired a searcher to find my birth parents?"

"I don't remember you telling us that," Mom said.

"I did tell you," I said.

"She told you," Bob vouched. "I was there."

"Anyway, yes?" Mom said.

"Well, we found my birth parents."

Silence.

I don't remember being told I was adopted. It was never an event, it was just something I always knew. But the expectation in a '70s adoption was that my own curiosity about my original parents who made me should not exceed that of my parents who raised me. My dad called them my "biological" parents, which made them sort of like fruit flies to me, not people who could be found or who really have much significance in my life past the initial act of creation.

I honored this unspoken and never-acknowledged agreement for most of my life. My parents survived two life-threatening illnesses apiece while I was a teenager, and I thought it was inappropriate at the time and for many years after to even admit the slightest bit of interest in my "bios", even to myself. But when I started becoming aware of what I didn't know, I discovered a vast, overwhelming, cavernous darkness that opened up a realization of how much of me was missing from my own self-knowledge, and I couldn't pretend any more that it was all right.

"That's wonderful," Mom said, trying to be positive and supportive. "I mean, I think it's wonderful. Is it wonderful?" She had a thing about not projecting too much forced enthusiasm on an event without finding out the facts.

"It's complicated," I replied. "I thought the searcher might be able to locate my birth father first because we knew from the agency's narrative that he's Orthodox and from the South. How many Orthodox Jews are there in the South?"

"What's a narrative?" my mom asked.

I explained it to her again. Because birth and adoption records are sealed in New York State—and in most states—my adoption agency was not permitted to share any "identifying information" with me from my own records. Here I'd thought I could waltz in and access my files when I was ready, but I was dead wrong. Instead, the social worker created what they call a "narrative" from my file: my history, ancestry, and birth information is redacted of anything specific, and I got a cozy, continuous tale woven from the wreckage.

I was told that my birth father and mother were originally from the "southeastern region of the United States," which narrows it down to thirteen possible states. This "narrative" is based on decades-old notes made by the original social workers and then reinterpreted through the subjective lens of the current social worker. Why can a random social worker know everything about me while I am left in the dark?

"It turns out that my birth father is from Miami, and his whole family is still there," I said. Miami was only four hours away from where we all sat at that very moment.

"Have you contacted him?" my mom asked.

"The sad thing is, he passed away a few years ago."

"I'm sorry," Mom said.

"He passed away a year after I started my search. If the records had been open, I may have had the opportunity to meet him."

"What about your biological mother?" Dad asked.

"I was able to find her on my own, with the information my searcher provided. She's living in Ireland."

"Ireland!" my mom exclaimed.

"She's the executive assistant to an Irish Nobel Laureate. They do global peace work for children. Most of the family lives in Pensacola now." Eight hours away from where we were now. In fact, we just happened to be smack dab in the middle of my two newly found geographic ancestral outposts.

"Have you spoken to her?"

"Briefly," I said.

"Are you going to meet her?" Mom asked.

"I hope to."

"But you don't want a relationship with her, you just want to meet her, right?" Dad asked. It was really less of a question and more of a statement.

"I don't know," I lied, undermining my whole open-book policy for this conversation.

"Is there anything else?" my mom asked.

"I have two maternal uncles, a grandmother, and a brother."

"You mean half-brother," she corrected.

"I think you just say brother. It's kinder."

"Just take this slow. We don't want you getting hurt."

I wanted to say: I'm already hurt. Can't you see all the missing pieces—the medical and genetic history, the ancestry, my very own story, the real narrative before I was slipped into your loving arms?

"I promise to take it slow. But I have an opportunity here to get a lot of my questions answered. The missing pieces you take for granted when you grow up in your biological family." I used my dad's word, but he stayed silent. "You know that this has nothing to do with anyone being replaced. You are my parents and you are not replaceable."

"Well, this is really wonderful," Mom said. "We have extended family now."

That "we" was all I needed to hear.

i'

Passing a Parent
Nikki MacCallum

T'S NOT UNTIL I'M CLOSING IN on him that I realize the man hobbling slowly in front of me along the path beside the Cape Cod Canal is my father. Feeling more shocked than surprised, I stop running about fifteen feet behind him, begin jogging in place, and look at him. His legs look brittle, like he could be knocked over if a bike passed too close to him or if the wind blew too hard. He does not look like a man who has run thirty-two marathons, including Boston in two hours and forty-six minutes. He ran those thirty-two marathons when he was in his thirties and forties, before he embarked on a nearly twenty-year-long battle with alcoholism.

When I arrived on the Cape last night, for a weekend visit, he was already in bed. My mom warned me that his walking has gotten worse. Years of alcohol abuse have given him permanent nerve damage. I got up early this morning and decided to go for a run, secretly hoping to avoid seeing him. Plus, I wanted to get in a training today because I've only got two months left until my first marathon.

I have a love-hate relationship with running. Actually, I hate it, but I'm oddly addicted to it. Really, all it's gotten me are some free t-shirts, a lot of shin splints, and something to share with my dad. We used to run together on this very strip of land when I was a little girl. I was always frustrated that I couldn't keep up and I'd fake assorted sports injuries, hoping to get his permission to slow down.

Now I'm afraid to pass him. I continue jogging in place, trying to stay with the beat of Lady Gaga's "The Edge of Glory," playing on my iPod. My dad stops moving forward completely and coughs, trying to catch his breath. He looks old and fragile and breakable. I watch him struggle, and for a second his condition feels like justice to me. After all, he did this to himself: wrecked his ability to walk, not to mention run, and ruined his career as an attorney. He completely self-destructed.

My mother had to pay all the bills on her music-teacher salary: his medical bills, office bills, bills from car accidents and unnecessary parking tickets. I've watched him die so many deaths, yet he's still here. Suddenly, I'm angry that I have to stop behind him and see him this way, that *I'm* the one who's running in place. My anger turns to annoyance that I'm losing valuable seconds on account of him; when you're training for a marathon, every second counts. He taught me that. Can't he just go faster so I can go faster?

My annoyance turns to guilt. It must be difficult for him to barely be able to do something he once loved and did so successfully. I don't want to rub that in, to cause him shame, by passing him. How would it make him feel to have me—the daughter who used to fake shin splints to get out of running with him because she couldn't keep up—pass him, and not because she's fast now? Then again, I can't jog in place forever.

Guilt turns to compassion. This is the same man who took me running every Saturday as a little girl, on this very same seven-mile stretch of land. The man who coached my middle-school soccer team and even let me dress him up as a woman for Halloween one year. This is my friend and dad. Now here I am, training for my first marathon, following in his footsteps. For that, I'm proud.

Up until this moment, even with all his drinking and self-destructing, I've always thought of my father as immortal. His outfit today features a pair of spandex, neon yellow shorts that shouldn't be worn by anyone over the age of twenty. He's always tried to dress the way he thinks young people do. It wasn't until I was twelve that I realized my dad had turned twenty-seven for the past six consecutive birthdays.

I guess you always know that, in the circle of life, your parents will grow weaker and you'll grow stronger, and a moment will come when you'll trade places with them. But I never imagined it happening quite like this. Maybe I'm afraid to pass him because I don't want it to be true. I'm no longer the child in this relationship. And I can't give him back his legs.

He loses his balance for a moment and stumbles on the path, and I'm surprised that my instinct isn't to run and help him; instead, I feel paralyzed, as if my own legs don't work. It comes to me that I'm not supposed to help him. The greatest gift I can give him, as unnatural as it feels, is to pass him.

In this second, I realize, I totally accept him for who he is, with all the drinking and everything that went with it. Maybe not permanently, maybe not even an hour from now. But for just this moment, I'm okay with it all, free of resentment. Because I love my father, I will do what he can no longer do himself.

I turn up Lady Gaga as loud as she can go, and I run. I don't look at him when I pass him. I don't know that it's ever easy to pass a parent. All I can do is the one thing he taught me. *Run.*

i

Jason's Story

Carl Ballenas

JASON ALWAYS SEEMED TO NEED EXTRA TIME with his school-work. He came to my attention when he entered my fifth-grade class. He did not seem focused and would often look out the window.

When he took a test, he would be only halfway finished when time ran out. His mother was concerned and hoped that he would grow out of it. He made it through the year and was now in my sixth-grade homeroom class, but he continued to have a difficult time with his work. Jason required a lot of patience, and with so many students, patience was not always available.

I gave my students a project: they were to write their own books. The Nationwide book company donated a book kit for each student. The company would bind each manuscript with a hard cover, making it look like a real library book. Students took the task to heart and created little masterpieces. Each book needed eight pages of text with some pages for illustrations. They could use photos, but they had to be scanned. I allotted them six weeks to finish. Proofreading created a lot of extra work for me. I set a date to read first drafts and another date when the finished manuscripts had to be packed up and sent to the printer.

Jason told me he had a hard time thinking of anything to write. Some students were writing about fantastic space battles in make-believe worlds and others were writing about their favorite vacations to distant lands. I began asking Jason, on a daily basis, to see his first draft, but the answer was always the same. I told him to write something that was personal, something he knew about. He looked more confused than ever. I had run out of patience.

Finally, on the day before the manuscripts were to be shipped out, Jason came up to my desk with a stack of crumpled pages—his first draft. I was horrified at the thought of reading it, making corrections, and then getting him to complete it. When I saw that he had glued pictures to the paper and had not scanned them, I took the pages from him and told him it was too late. I scolded him for procrastinating and sent him back to his seat.

With a deep sigh, I picked up the pages even as I thought that checking his story would be impossible. No way could I find the time to help him. I dreaded looking through it, but glanced at the cover. On it was the title, *The Little Boy Who Lost His Father*. Included was a drawing of a butterfly with a sad frown on its face and a cloud with tears falling to the ground. I stared at it and began to feel a pain in my soul. On the next page he had written, "Based on a true story."

I looked up and saw Jason seated at his desk, looking out the window. As I read it, I did not notice the misspelled words, the incorrect grammar, or the glue oozing from the edge of the pictures. There were pictures of Jason as a baby and one with his father holding him in his arms. Another showed Jason in his mother's arms, crying and looking at a birthday cake.

He had written, "One day a little boy woke up and felt something was wrong. He heard silence in the whole house. He did not understand. His mother was in tears and then he noticed that the one true person who ever meant anything to him was not there. He asked his mommy, where was his daddy. She replied, "Son, he is in a better place."

The book continued with stories of scary dreams and waking up in the middle of the night screaming out, "Daddy!" His mother told him to recite Philippians 4:13: "I can do all things through Him who strengthens me." Repeating this verse over and over, he was finally able to sleep.

He wrote about asking God to allow him to speak to his father, if only for one minute, so he could say things he never got a chance to say before he died, or to give him a hug good-bye. On his fifth birthday, he was so sad that he refused to accept any gifts and would not blow out the candles on his cake or even eat it. Nothing else was on his mind but getting that last chance to be with his father.

When he turned eight years old, things began to change, and he started to get used to the feelings of emptiness. He felt that he would always have a hole in his heart, but he tried to make peace with himself. When he looked at his mother, he saw her pain, especially when he misbehaved or didn't do well in school.

On the last page, Jason wrote, "Finally, as the boy grew up and became mature, he knew what to do when someone you love is gone. He knew that one day he and his father would be together again. He also knew that his father watched over him every day and would never leave his side. So the boy never actually lost his father. They were only separated for a little while."

After regaining my composure, I called Jason up to my desk. He told me he had written a personal story and had not even told his mother about it. I helped him correct his spelling and grammar, and I scanned his pictures. He had only seven pages of text; he needed to write one more, so I suggested he write a letter to his father.

Dear Father, I wish I could see you for one last time. What have you been doing? I want to ask you so many questions. I am a big boy now and I am in the sixth grade. I play sports like basketball and football. Mom is doing great so far, and I am being the man of the house and taking care of her. I can't wait to see you again one day. Your son, Jason. PS I love you!

Few dry eyes remained when anyone read Jason's book. His mother told me that she did not know he had written the story, and it had caused a profound impact at home. Her husband's relatives had thought Jason had forgotten his father, but when they read the book, it succeeded in bringing the family closer. The book got the attention of a local TV station, and they asked Jason to read parts of his book on the air for Father's Day. While his mother and I spoke about how the book had evolved, I noticed the crew took him into their hearts. I saw a confidence and joy in Jason that I had not seen before.

Jason has moved on, and although he continues to struggle with his schoolwork, he has improved. And from time to time, he still looks out the window.

i

·····································

A Daughter's Forgiveness and The Ripple Effect

Jessie Fahay

'LL BE HONEST—when folks ask me for a personal, inspirational story, I have a difficult time thinking of what that might be. A part of me feels as though my journey and how I got to where I am in show business may come off as too whiney or typical.

I was a frustrated actress. What actor hasn't wished things could be easier? I'd like to meet that person. But I didn't just want to be famous—I'm someone who has always had an interest in participating in theatre arts that make a difference. I had seen a lot of powerful productions in the past that I thought could really support sustainable change, if they raised awareness for a certain cause or were aimed to educate. That is where the idea of my not-for-profit theatre company,

Ripple Effect Artists, came along. But what is the personal unleashing story from my own past? I had to dig deep to think about this one.

What is it that makes an organization work? Communication. Dedication. Hard work. Perseverance. Blah Blah. Blah. This is stuff we already know. Here is what I propose. An organization—and furthermore, the richness of one's life—is dependent on the quality of one thing and one thing only: relationships. How much we can trust each other within a company, as well as being open, allowing for times of vulnerability, being able to ask for assistance, and being able to work together, is determined by the quality of relationships.

The birth of Ripple Effect Artists Inc. was able to happen because of one of my own personal relationships being completely transformed. One relationship in particular is now with someone with whom I work extremely closely and who is one of the most active board members of the organization. Five years ago, if you had told me I would be working diligently with this woman, I would have said to you, "Well, I love her, but I don't think I could ever work with her." This woman is none other than … my mother.

Our relationship throughout my early twenties was fine. We got along great. We spoke pretty often. Yet, there was a block in my ability to be completely open with her. Why? Incidents from the past, of course—things that cannot be erased or corrected. So what do most human beings do? We hold on. We carry around all the anger and resentment that may come with those incidents.

See, we had a tumultuous history, my mom and me. If you were to meet her now, you would have no idea that she would even be capable of these things—yet, they happened. Like any mother, she had her times of stress, worry, and frustration with her only daughter, whom she loved. How did that stress manifest? I got hit in public. What happened in my adolescent years? I was told I was too overweight. As an adult, I thought I had pushed these many awful incidents out of my memory, but they lurked. And the child inside of me felt the need for protection from the danger of my past.

One day, it all shifted. Someone set an example from me. I witnessed a young lady get on the phone and forgive her father for leaving her and her mother at a young age. When I asked why she did that, she replied, "I wanted to live a life where I am not constantly afraid that someone will leave." So what did I do? I got on the phone.

"Mom, this is really hard—but I've been holding on to resentment due to the negative comments you made about my appearance and also that you hit me as a child. I am telling you now that I forgive you. I do not agree with what you did—but I can forgive it."

And then I heard silence. My thoughts were racing. *Did I just screw things up? Did I make her upset? Am I going to regret bringing up these past events? What did I do?*

And then I heard her voice choked with tears: "I could not have asked for a better gift for my sixtieth birthday."

And in that moment, I realized what all the religious fanatics go crazy over—forgiveness. Did this make me born again? No. It made me realize the power of forgiveness, completion, and closure in a way that I had never discovered before. From this, I got the ability to receive my mother's love. I was able to communicate with her with complete honesty and vulnerability.

A couple of months later, I made another scary phone call. "Mom, I want to be a producer and start a theatre company that makes a difference. We need resources. We need money." Her response: "I am ready to write a check."

Since this conversation, Ripple Effect Artists Inc. has become incorporated and has mounted six well-reviewed productions that have raised funds and awareness for multiple advocacy groups. We have also conducted readings and five different major fundraising events.

We have a staff of four, a board of thirteen, and an ensemble of twenty-eight actors and directors. There have been several news articles about us in various theatre news outlets. We have an event space and an office. We have artists and business professionals committed to using theatre as a vehicle to provoke dialogue and move audiences from apathy to action. We are a community committed to greatness while making an impact, all based on thriving and positive relationships.

And it all started from the transformation of an incredibly special relationship. My amazing mother is my best friend and my angel in life who has supported this company through all its journeys. None of this could have happened without her.

Count the Waves:
Fighting Tradition and Trusting My Intuition
Mary C. Harris

HOW DO TWO PEOPLE fall in love? Many believe that love happens due to convenience or coincidence. Others feel that people grow into love. My story is a bit ... different.

During the summer of 2004, I had my heart broken. I cared deeply for someone who truly wasn't right for me. Little did I know that this situation would become the catalyst for my most profound adventure.

Once I was ready to move on from that chapter in my life, I made a list of goals I planned on achieving. One was to travel, and Hawaii was at the top of the list. I reached out to two college friends to see if they wanted to take a trip with me, and they agreed. Destination: Oahu.

March 2005 arrived, and a week before I was scheduled to leave, I was involved in an accident where a minivan rear-ended my car. An ambulance brought me to a nearby hospital, and I was hurt badly enough that an eleven-hour flight to Hawaii was out of the question. Needless to say, I was devastated. Luckily, my friends were willing to wait for me to get better, so we postponed our trip until May.

When I was at my parents' house recovering, I distinctly remember my mother saying, "Everything happens for a reason. I know that there was a reason that you were in this car accident. One day you will know." She's been right so often in my life (other than the time she was dead wrong about cutting my bangs in second grade) and she was right about this.

May arrived quicker than I had anticipated and Hawaii was a dream—85 degrees, sunny, clear water, breathtaking. During one of our first evenings there, my friends and I went to a nightclub a few blocks away from the beach.

We split off at one point, and when I found them again, they were speaking to someone. He was handsome and tall, about 6'1", clean-cut and well-dressed, with an honest, kind smile and beautiful blue eyes. "Mary, this is Cody. He's a Marine, and this is his first week back from his deployment." Our eyes connected and we gazed at each other for a brief moment and smiled.

"Well, it was nice meeting you. It's getting late, so we are going to get going." My friends began to make their way toward the exit. I thought to myself: *How could I leave? I have to do something.* My intuition or a higher power was nudging me to say something. *This could not end here.*

So, thinking as quickly as I could, I gave Cody a phone number to reach us and suggested that we all go snorkeling or grab a bite to eat with some of his friends. And then I walked away. *Right, Mary. Snorkeling. You just met the guy. Let's put uncomfortable, red im-*

print-inducing masks on our faces. If he goes through with it, this could be like a flashback to high school chemistry class. I'll go get the Bunsen burner.

The next morning, Cody actually called and we made group plans. He and I spent time together over the next several days. During one of our dates, he held my hand and put his arm around me. One night when we were alone, I kissed him outside my hotel room. It was the perfect kiss, the best of my life (so far). The next night he asked me if I wanted to go for a walk on the beach, just the two of us. He held my hand and we walked barefoot along the shoreline and talked for hours. I felt safe with him—as though I had known him my whole life. And as crazy as it sounds, something told me we were meant for each other.

Our week together was short-lived, and I had to go back home to New Jersey. When I arrived at the airport to depart, I saw a familiar smile. Cody surprised me. We sat together outside the terminal. My friends took some pictures of Cody and I saying good-bye, and I began to feel tears welling up in my eyes. He held me close until I had to leave.

"I know this may sound strange," Cody said, "but you're the girl of my dreams. I feel as though I am losing my best friend, and I just found her. I don't care what I need to do to make this work; I'm willing to do it. I know you live on the other side of the country, and we're many miles apart, but I would do anything to make you happy and make our relationship work."

Saying good-bye and getting on that plane was one of the most difficult things I have ever done. When I landed in New Jersey and turned on my cell phone, I had a voicemail from Cody: "You're on the plane now. I just want you to know that I miss you already, and you are beautiful."

After a week, he asked me to come back to Hawaii and live there for the rest of the summer. Against the advice and wishes of my parents, family, and friends, I followed my heart and my intuition and I went back to Oahu to be with Cody. That summer, I experienced the purest, most genuine love. And I learned that everything does happen for a reason.

Cody and I got married in December of 2005 and had our five-year vow renewal in 2010. Whenever I visit a beach, I think of our love story. An ocean's waves are infinite, and our love feels that way to me.

Everyone's love story is different and special, and there are countless ways that love can take shape. For Cody and me, it took just a moment. Everything does happen for a reason—even getting rearended by a minivan.

The Real Story of Aladar

Kelly Wilson

THERE I STOOD, with feelings of helplessness almost impossible to avoid. In the center of my son Collin's bedroom, I stood still while Collin kicked my shins in the same yellowed spots that he had bruised last week. He was screaming "I hate you" and "you're stupid" in a voice that sounded so frightening it had occasionally prompted my neighbors to call the police.

Wishing I had kept the upstairs window closed on this hot summer day, I had to force myself to let go of the fear of my neighbors and their actions so I could focus on Collin. As he continued to scream at me, I kept telling Collin quietly and calmly, "I love you." Tears streamed down my face.

I'd like to say I was crying because of the physical pain that comes from being kicked in the same bruised places, but the reality was more related to that feeling of helplessness—I was trying to help Collin, but

I wasn't impacting his behavior enough. At age five, it was challenging to get him to his room. What would I do when he was sixteen or twenty, and much bigger than me? Would I need to be afraid of him? Panic set in.

The tantrum had begun downstairs when Collin took a Matchbox car from his younger brother, Sean. Not only had he wrenched the car from Sean's hand, but he'd hit him as well. I had to do something, so I took Collin to his room, and a full-blown tantrum erupted. Standing there instead of making dinner, I knew I needed to shift my focus from what I was feeling to what I could do to help Collin. I wasn't reaching him. I wondered, *What am I missing?*

I had been focused on teaching Collin exactly what he was supposed to be doing—you know, the appropriate behavior. Sometimes Collin used new skills, but sometimes he did not. Because Collin could repeat what he was supposed to do, and could sometimes do it, many told me he was being manipulative. Certainly he knew the rules and how to ask for a toy, and yes, he could repeat them. Yet he did not seem to get why the rules were important. That is what I was missing—how to teach the importance. I needed something concrete, something Collin could relate to.

I was now staring at the ceiling with my thoughts swirling, still unable to stop my own tears, with Collin still kicking and screaming. Then Collin made a noise that reminded me of his favorite movie, a Disney movie called "Dinosaur." An idea popped into my head and I began speaking.

As you may know, Disney movies create good and evil with such clarity, there is no crossover. The good guy is remarkably good, and the bad guy is totally bad. Hoping this example might be concrete, I said firmly, "Collin, is Krone kind and nice? Or is he mean? Does anyone like Krone? Does he have friends? Does he use nice words? Does anyone hug him? Does his mom cook him dinner and smile at him?" Okay, so the mom cooking dinner part was totally based on the fact that I needed to make dinner an hour ago.

Pausing to chuckle at myself, I noticed the quiet. Collin had completely stopped; it was like he was on pause. *OMG*—I thought—*I just discovered the magic kid-remote controller and hit pause.* I looked down to see what Collin was doing. And then it happened ...

Collin looked up at me and said "Mommy, I want to be Aladar!" Then he began to cry giant crocodile tears, and he reached out to me for a hug. As you may have guessed, Krone was the classic bad-guy dinosaur, and Aladar was the exceptional good-guy dinosaur. But I hadn't even mentioned Aladar. And I really did not think Collin was listening to me anyway. Somehow, it happened—Collin made the connection, a great breakthrough, with the help of a Disney movie. He got it.

I fell to the floor and held onto my Collin. Though he and I cried, I knew that an important correlation had been made. Something had clicked. I saw it, I felt it. Collin had made a connection between his actions and consequences. Hitting people was being like Krone, while asking for a toy using nice words was being like Aladar. This affected the way others treated you. He understood empathy and understanding. Now Collin and I had a foundation to work from. He could learn about making choices—Aladar vs. Krone choices, of course. The moment was magical and of the greatest importance!

When you experience an event like this, you know immediately that your life is going to be different. It is epic. This was a game-changer and one of our most celebrated accomplishments. This was so important, it immediately affected his demeanor; instantly, I knew I would not need to be afraid of Collin growing up.

Collin is now twenty and still has Fragile X Syndrome and Attention Deficit Hyperactivity Disorder (ADHD). Yet he brings such positive energy to all. I knew that hot summer day, when I was sitting on Collin's floor and hugging him, that he would be okay.

I guess the "magic" of Disney exists in my family; it just looks a little different. But then, many things in our family are magical, even though they look a little different.

i'
······························
Perfectionists Anonymous
Elaine Taylor-Klaus

"HI, MY NAME IS ELAINE and I am a recovering perfectionist." I now know that failure is as excellent a teacher as success, but gaining that knowledge took a lot more than twelve steps.

I was raised as part of the achievement elite, with Ivy-League expectations provided in utero and ambition deeply ingrained. Ambivalent about anything average, one thing was always clear: failure was not an option.

On the surface, the "achievement establishment" worked for me. I looked great on paper, a high achiever with academic success and post-graduate honors.

Yet I had an inauthentic relationship with success. Avoidance of failure governed my decision-making. I never did anything I didn't do well. I limited opportunities that wouldn't maximize achievement, choosing only those challenges I had a strong chance to win.

While there is something to be said for taking a strength-based approach to life, the truth is that I let fear of striking out prevent me from playing the game.

I would likely have continued on that course, unabated, passing those achievement expectations down to the next generation, had I not been gifted with a child who was challenged by the complexities of life and learning.

My daughter's path was destined to depart from mine. She has been my greatest teacher, despite my initial reluctance to be her student.

For years, I danced around the edges of my child's challenges, buying therapies to enable her to fit into my vision of what it meant for a "smart kid" to be successful. Her failure to thrive in school reflected my failure as a parent, and that was not acceptable.

I thought I was leading her—albeit dragging her, kicking and screaming—to her own success. But no matter how hard I tried, it wasn't her path. And yet, all I could see was my own "failure" to produce a carbon copy of myself, to produce the next generation's agent for the achievement elite.

At some point during her elementary school years, I learned the most powerful lesson of my life: to be "successful" as her parent, I had to stop trying to "fix" her so that she could meet my expectations. She wasn't, in fact, broken. I had to let her follow her own path and stop forcing her to try to excel on mine.

That meant redefining success based on her gifts and talents, and adjusting my expectations based on what was important for her.

It's empowering to strive for excellence, and that is a value I continue to hold and teach my children. But to expect excellence in all aspects of life, with little or no room for failure, is perfectionism. And that takes a psychic toll on any human existence.

As parents, the best way we can support our kids is by accepting them and empowering them to embrace and accept themselves. We do not serve them by letting them feel broken if they do not achieve everything they attempt. When we teach them to avoid failures, we teach them not to take risks. We teach them to be less than human— because we humans spend a lot more time making mistakes than we do being perfect.

To embrace, and accept, and truly be okay with all that it means to be human, we must teach our children to "fail forward" in life and to learn from mistakes as part of their human experience.

Failure gets a bad rap. We don't walk without falling, or talk without babbling. And yet somehow, we teach our youth to avoid mistakes at all costs.

What if we actually embraced our moments of human frailty as an opportunity for growth, instead of fighting them? What if we saw as much opportunity in failure as we do in success?

Researchers tell us that resilience is a stronger predictor of "success" than many other expected factors (like opportunity). But how does one learn resilience? We experience failure, and we learn to deal with it. In other words, the secret to success is in failure.

The time has come to redefine what success looks like, to renegotiate our relationship with perfection, and reacquaint ourselves with "good enough."

And what does it look like to redefine success?

… pursuing excellence, not perfection

… embracing "good enough," and

… selecting where to put our attention, instead of assuming we should pay attention to everything—and then chiding ourselves for falling short.

Ultimately, redefining success means setting our own expectations instead of looking to the outside world to define them for us. And it means basing those expectations on our values and our passions rather than on some prescribed societal norms that tell us what we are "supposed" to do.

I'm a recovering perfectionist. There is a part of me that will always be tempted by perfection, but every day, I make the effort to redefine success in terms that makes sense for me and my family.

Instead of expecting excellence in every aspect of life:

- I encourage my dyslexic daughter to be proud of a B on a Lit paper.
- I remind my husband, who judges his own performance too harshly, that a 90 is still an A.
- I own my mistakes vocally, and I forgive myself … a lot.

And that little girl who taught me so much?

She is an independent young woman now, pursuing her dream to be an actor. She is wildly successful by any standards we might use to evaluate. It's not the plan I would have laid out for her. In truth, it is better than anything I ever could have imagined. She is happy, healthy, and passionately pursuing her dreams.

That is what I call success.

i'
....
Adventures in Caregiving
Josh Rivedal

FEW THINGS INVOKE a more vehement denial than when your Significant-Other tells you they've just been diagnosed with cancer. Yes, denial—not just a river in Egypt.

"Bah, humbug. You're definitely an Aquarius, not a Cancer, you silly goose."

But when Significant-Other's tears didn't stop, I knew that life had just changed, shifted, and become both a bit more real and surreal all at the same time.

An entire spectrum of thoughts immediately surged to the forefront. What is she going to do? What am I going to do? I'm happy to take care of her as best I can—but damn, it's gonna be a lot of work. Why her? Why me?

Significant-Other had an especially difficult roller coaster of emotions—her mother had died from cancer a few years back, her lovely but hairless cat had died from cancer the year prior, and her best friend was in the process of dying from an especially nasty cancer, extinguishing a flame that should have shone brightly for at least another thirty years.

However, Significant-Other made a smart decision at the very beginning. She reached out to her friends and her especially Brave-Sister on my behalf, to help me help her. I couldn't do it all alone, and she knew that the prospect of doing so would break me in two.

The coming weeks were filled with doctor's appointments, second opinions, paperwork, and scheduling surgery. Finally, the doctors found a small tumor at the base of her tongue.

After a wee *bairn* of a Scottish doctor resected (fancy word for "sliced out") a three-centimeter piece of the back of her tongue, she was on pain drugs galore. Many of them made her an irritable, nauseous mess, which then brought on a terrible and persistent anxiety, the likes of which I had never before seen.

I knew how to deal with *my* anxiety. I speak about it in front of hundreds at a time, after which people will pull me aside to discuss their own anxiety. I get to hug them and be with them one-on-one for a few minutes. But how was I supposed to deal with the anxiety of Significant-Other for an undetermined period of time?

Significant-Other's anxiety was a true test of my patience, not to mention my mental health. Self-coaching, a call to a therapist friend, and honest conversations with Significant-Other were exactly what the doctor ordered to make my life and caregiving a bit more manageable.

Never once did I think Significant-Other would die from the diagnosis or the treatment. But the emotional baggage that one accumulates in the interim is heavy enough to make some sink for good.

Why do these things happen? Who the hell knows? Spending your life trying to gauge whether God is fair or unjust—or wondering whether the government is out to get you with cancerous crop pesticides—is about as useful as chasing your own tail.

Hindsight does provide a luxury: the ability to wax poetic on any set of circumstances. With the benefit of clearer vision—and with Significant-Other's successful cancer treatment in the rear-view mirror—it's a bit easier to see that the whole ordeal was not and still is not easy to understand in the slightest. I have to squint my eyes and focus on the bits I want to see, the ones that help me move forward, to heal and to help others. I get to choose my own viewpoint and my own adventure.

The purpose I take away from things like Significant-Other's cancer—and my own brush with suicide in the past—is that it's all about refinement, at least for me. I already won the "white guy born in the United States of America" lottery, so that skews things a bit. I get to learn something from this—or at least I get to try.

I learned how to ask for help, which is something I still struggle with at times. Significant-Other asked for help from Brave-Sister and her friends, which in turn helped me find a way to ask my own friends and even Significant-Other for help while I played the role of caregiver.

I learned about grace and dignity. Three of my grandparents had died from cancer before I was born. I don't worry about it, but there's a good chance I'll probably get it, too (sweet b'jesus, let it be something confined to my pinky toenail, if anything at all). I now have a better idea of how to ask for help for myself and how to navigate the healthcare system.

I learned how to find my funny, even in the face of a s&*+ storm.

And even though Significant-Other and I are no longer together I learned to how better love myself and my friends, and I learned patience.

I learned.

i'

....

Physical Health

"*Health... is not so much a state, but a force: the power to resist and overcome threats to one's well-being.*"
  - Gregory P. Fields

Silence is Golden

Natalie Roy

I HAVE RECENTLY FOUND MYSELF SPEECHLESS. Literally. All my life, I have chosen paths, relationships, and a career that revolve around my creative expression and my ability to communicate. So when I was faced with the cold reality of losing my voice, I also quite honestly lost myself.

I woke up on a rainy Sunday morning, after a night out on the town, feeling young and invincible, only to find that I could not speak. Though alarming—as I had never experienced this before in my entire career as an actor, singer, and teacher—I assumed after a day or two of rest, all would be well. Days later, when I was still unable to speak, I began to panic. I consulted a specialist and was given an aggressive round of antibiotics and steroids. I was assured my voice would be back in a few days. I was told to rest.

Although it was the last thing I wanted to do, I thought, sure, why not? A few days "vacation" and I'll be back in action. But by Day Five of silence, I officially hit rock bottom.

It may seem dramatic that, less than a week after losing my voice, I would be sobbing uncontrollably at 3 a.m., scared, alone, and full of anxiety. But this breakdown was also my breakthrough. It really had nothing to do with my voice at all; it had to do with my self-value. It had to do with love.

There is a beautiful quote from Rumi I recently stumbled across while I was sitting at home, starring at the walls, feeling sad and lost and sorry for myself: "The wound is the place where the Light enters you." It's amazing to me how life seems to hand us lessons on a silver platter, if only we are willing to slow down and be present to them— or in my case, when we are forced to.

I ran a hot bath, lit some candles, and crawled under the water, my face still drenched with tears. As I let myself be held by the warmth of the water and let my soundless cries flow, without resistance, I saw so clearly that I hadn't lost anything physical (although I had, of course). What I had really lost was my identity.

I had spent my life doing, giving, working, contributing. I was a results-driven, accomplishing machine. I had done a lot with my life and my time thus far: I'd created a lot of relationships, lived in several cities, and worked as an actress in many roles. I'd written a book and become a yoga teacher. I graduated post-secondary education with high honors, sang and performed across North America, and moved to New York City.

But even while doing all of those things, I always carried a private, secret sadness. It would rear its ugly head every time I stopped having the next job, the next adventure, the next thing to do. In the silence of my life—the downtime, the space between—lay a deep restlessness. I felt unhappiness, a sense of lack, and the need to move and to do more.

And suddenly, as I lay alone in the quiet of my small, pink bathroom, I felt it all, like a giant weight of desperation. It had a name: "not enough."

I was the girl whom everyone would assume had it all—the wonderful family, the perfect husband, the great career. But I was so afraid to admit to myself, and feel, what my wise body knew: that I had kept myself far too busy to have to deal with the reality, and I felt that I was not enough.

As if the bathwater covering my body was a wave of truth, I suddenly knew what I had spent my life doing. Doing. Me, Natalie—the energy, the spirit, the human—was simply not enough. Not enough to warrant being loved, appreciated, or valued. That's why I had to take action. I had to DO things to make myself more worthy, because whatever I was, it was simply was not up to par.

I saw all the ways I had filled up the world with my actions and not with myself. If I can just do the right things, say the right things, make people feel good about themselves, contribute to the world in some way—*then* I'll deserve to be here, and *then* I'll deserve to be happy. And *then* I'll love myself.

I lost my voice, but what I found was far greater. I found a scared, flawed, insecure little human being longing to be accepted and loved—and then I realized I had found us all.

We all are desperately craving connection. We come out of the womb and the only thing we know is that we need to connect. We know we will literally die otherwise. As we grow up, we learn many other things, but perhaps this remains the thing that matters most.

As I lay in that bath (which was now growing cold), I placed my hands over my chest and cried a river of tears. I let go of all the fear. I embraced it. I stopped pretending it wasn't there, and I stopped feeling like it was bad or wrong. I just let it be. Incredibly, I finally found what I had been chasing: I found love and acceptance and validation, because I was able to give those things to myself.

I don't know where this quote came from, or who said it, but as I journey through each day now, I carry it with me: "In what fields did I sow seeds to deserve so very, very much? And the answer came, you were born deserving."

We are born deserving. There is nothing to do, there is only to be. And it is enough.

Live Courageously

Mariagrazia Buttitta

ORN AND RAISED IN SICILY, I was devastated to find out, five years ago, that I would be denied the opportunity in Sicily to pursue my dream of a college education in communication studies and creative writing. It was because of my disability.

While this would discourage many, my parents and I made an important decision to move to New Jersey to search for new opportunities. Despite my "different ability," New Jersey—specifically, The College of New Jersey—provided me with an equal opportunity to succeed in my studies. That also gave me hope that I was a step closer to fulfilling my dream: to never let my different ability stop me from achieving goals.

I was born with a rare eye condition called Cone Rod Dystrophy. This ocular disorder causes total blindness when I'm in contact with bright lights. My whole life, I had tried to hide who I was, because I felt sorry for myself. I started giving myself a pretend role of being someone I was not. Maybe I could fool people, but the sad part was that I was only fooling myself.

I never wanted people to see me as someone who was weak and suffering or who needed help. I decided to live in silence, because maybe if I ignored it enough, things would get better. Instead, they only got worse, and I became a miserable person.

I was in denial, depressed and hopeless. I started believing that I was a mistake in this world. I wanted to overcome my disability, but in truth, this wasn't about overcoming a disease or mental illness; it was about learning to first adapt, accept, and acknowledge who I was. It was about letting go of my fears and letting this voice inside of me be free.

When I got accepted to college in New Jersey, I should have been happy—but I still wasn't. I had risen and overcome a huge obstacle, but I still had another (metaphorical) mountain to climb.

One of my favorite outdoor activities is going hiking with family and friends. I enjoy hiking at the Ramapo Mountain Reservation up in North Jersey. Once I finally reach the Overlook, I can sit back and enjoy the view, and then can begin meditating.

For most people, hiking can be a physical challenge. However, for me, it is more of a mental challenge. I know that I have to be alert and make sure my feet end up where they are supposed to be. My cane for the blind serves as a hiking stick, but it also helps me to keep my balance. I started hiking at a very young age, and I am passionate about it.

There are still moments when I wish to give up, but I have to constantly remind myself that hard work always results in a positive reward. I love the number of people I inspire along the way, and I am also very thankful for those who shout words of encouragements during my path. Hearing people cheer me on with "you are doing great" or "you can do this!" is always a wonderful feeling. And reaching the top of the mountain is a tremendous relief, because that means that my "blindness" is not interfering with my life.

My different ability does not define who I am. I am not my disability, I am not my anxiety, and I am not my depression.

Hiking has allowed me to realize that, though the path traveled might be a little bumpy, with hard work and persistence, one can achieve outstanding results. Today, I am extremely proud of who I've become. I do not see my different ability as a limitation, but rather as an opportunity for me to experience and see life from a different point of view. Life challenges should be seen as opportunities for growth.

A great attitude is everything in life. I am not saying I'm impervious to frustration or that my life is perfect. I still have many more hurdles to overcome, because I'm still a work in progress. But I have a great support system of family, friends, and professionals.

Help can come in many different forms, including simply talking about what I'm going through, writing, exercising, listening to music, meditating, traveling, and spending time with my dog, family, and friends. I know that by reaching out, I will never feel alone again, and I can continue to overcome any life challenge.

Bravery and success can be achieved simply by reaching out for help. Falling down and messing up has been a wonderful life lesson for me because it helps me to conquer my fears, and this has led me to become more resilient over time. I know things can be rough, but the trick to a better life is learning to be a good dancer. Life is all about rhythm and beat. You just have to learn how to dance to the different types of melodies. As I like to say, live life courageously.

i'

Following My Dreams Through the Valley of the Shadow of MS

Malini Singh McDonald

HERE ARE TWO FACTS ABOUT ME: I am dreamer and a goal-setter. That means that my dreams, for the most part, come true. I am a wonderful blend of the corporate professional and the free-spirited artist. As a New Yorker who does theatre, I've never dreamed of leaving home. That means that, in order to maintain my blended lifestyle, I choose to work a day job to support my art. I choose to have a nonstop schedule. I choose to live my life on my terms.

When a life-changing diagnosis presented itself, I fought against readjusting my life. After all, it has always been my life on my terms. No one and nothing dictated how I lived. My ego ran riot.

When I was diagnosed with multiple sclerosis in 2006, I decided to live in complete denial. How could this even happen? I have *dreams* and *goals*. I need my Broadway credit, to be published, to have a spiritual experience, to write poetry, and to get my PhD. That began my slow, downward spiral. I was exhausted. I was depressed. I couldn't see all the goodness of my life.

On February 14, 2006, my husband and I had just finished a productive planning meeting for our theatre season. As we walked up the icy hill, I felt three sharp pains on the left side of my body that stopped me in my tracks. Taking a deep breath, I held on to him as we continued to walk. Then it happened again. Same spot on the left side of my body. I figured it was the result of a misstep on the ice. Finally, we made it home.

The next morning, I woke up with blurriness in my right eye. I thought to myself, "Am I falling apart before the year really starts? I'm exhausted, there's pain in my side, and now my eye is blurry. I have theatre to do." I did what many would do in my situation: I bought an eyewash and Visine and hoped for the best.

I ran spotlight for a show that week. I was up in the balconies all alone. It was great. I was able to rest, watch the show, and hit my cues. I wasn't expecting this particular project to be easy, but I also wasn't expecting the sudden numbness on the left side of my body. I couldn't feel sensation on my face, arms, and legs. At that point, I thought maybe it would be best to see my doctor.

That began a weeklong visit with doctors for blood tests, brain scans and imaging, and neurological testing. The doctors ruled out Lyme disease and other related diseases. They were confident that my symptoms were consistent with MS. The one test that would have given them a true diagnosis was a spinal tap, but there was no way I was going to let them do that. As a result of my obstinacy, the doctors advised waiting for another exacerbation and then taking it from there.

That worked for me. After all, I didn't have MS! Eventually, the initial symptoms (pain, numbness, and optic neuritis) subsided, although my fatigue was constant. I chalked that up to my schedule. Not only was I working full-time, I was producing and directing three shows and starring in a TV show. I was beyond exhausted. I was beyond depressed. I was in pieces.

Then it happened again in August. The numbness and optic neuritis appeared on the *right* side of my body. I went back to the doctors, did the same tests, and still refused to do a spinal tap. However, my neurologist decided to move forward with the diagnosis and I began MS therapy in November 2006.

For the next few years, I slowly fell into a deep abyss of misery. I was emotionally, spiritually, mentally, physically, and financially vacant. One November evening in 2009, as I sat on my kitchen floor in my nighty, I decided I couldn't live the way I was living. I was done. I could either die or pull it together and ask for help. Guess what I chose?

Asking for help began a journey of reclamation. I tried my best to join the broken pieces of me as I slowly moved into acceptance. I hit a snag in 2010 when I couldn't afford my medication under my health plan. Instead of having a complete meltdown, I decided to adjust my approach to my health and wellness until I was able to adjust my health insurance. In accepting my reality, I changed my whole lifestyle to healthy living, which also boosted my emotional and spiritual condition.

Everything was fantastic. It was the best I'd felt in a long time, so I thought I should do a follow-up on my diagnosis with my neurologist. Maybe I didn't have MS. Then, as I was closing my show, I had another exacerbation. This time it came on hard with a lot of overall pain. I agreed to do another battery of blood tests, brain scans, neurological testing—and I said yes to the spinal tap.

The spinal tap confirmed that I did indeed have MS. I had to undergo treatment to relieve the symptoms. I was no longer in denial of my MS. I accepted it. I didn't like it, and I still don't like it, but I do accept it.

Living with MS means being in tune with my body and my mind and finding the perfectly imperfect balance. I am still a dreamer and goal-setter, but I balance it with relaxation and rejuvenation. I did get my Broadway credit. I have been published, I've had spiritual experiences, and I regularly write poetry.

The PhD is still a dream, but it has a future goal date. I don't have to do everything right this second. That's a fact, and I accept it … and I'm doing just fine.

i'

Tackling the Tough Stuff

Ali Stroker

WHEN I WAS TWO YEARS OLD and my brother was four, my entire family went through a traumatic car accident that left us all in a state of survival. My mom was driving us down the street to pick up something for my butterfly Halloween costume. Jake and I sat next to each other in the backseat of our Volkswagen when we were in a head-on collision.

Jake took the ambulance to the hospital and my mom and I rode in a police car. When we got to the hospital, Jake went into emergency surgery. They weren't sure if he was going to make it. That night, I had a spinal stroke in my bed and became paralyzed from the chest down. Soon enough, Jake and I met up again, side-by-side in the intensive care unit.

We came home from the hospital six months later, and we were two very different kids. My parents were certainly two different people as well. We had experienced an emotional and physical trauma that would change our perspectives forever. My physical identity would never be the same, because I no longer had the ability to feel from the chest down. I couldn't walk.

For the first ten years of my life, I was adapting to a new lifestyle of being in a wheelchair. I was learning to solve problems and hold back my tears of frustration and fear, in hopes that if I was "okay" then everyone else would be as well.

I was taught by my parents to see the glass half full, to find the positive and gift in every situation. I learned that pain and sadness are not good to let fester. As I move through my twenties, I'm realizing that running from my own despair makes things a lot harder.

Finding the light in situations is really helpful, but I had no clue what to do with my sadness, insecurities, pain, anger, and despair. I had never received any advice about how to handle these emotions, so I've decided to share a few things that have recently become very helpful while tackling the tough stuff:

- As an actress, I've learned that feelings are temporary. Trust that crying and letting out your pain will lead you to a new feeling, and most likely will lead to some kind of relief.

- When you don't think you can handle your own darkness, ask yourself, "Is there another perspective that I'm not seeing?" "What would it be like to look at this situation through someone else's eyes?"

- Finding a creative outlet allows you to not have to be solely reliant on another person and helps you move through your struggle. I have found that writing or putting on music and singing loudly helps me express myself. (I find this especially helpful with anger.)

- What you resist, persists. Avoiding the problems in your life will keep you stationary. Addressing your pain can feel like work, but actually, coming out on the other side with new realizations and confidence makes me feel like I've run a marathon.

- Don't let your mind continue to tell yourself the same story. Sometimes I can't break away from "the story" of what happened to me. Well, there's always another side to a story. Give yourself a break for a moment and tell yourself another side to the story. This will give you insight into the entire situation.

I never wanted anyone to see that I had major struggles. I used to think they were unattractive and no one would want to be around me if I shared anything negative. My new truth is that part of what makes me interesting is my darkness. The pain and challenges don't go away. New ones pop up all the time when you're ready to evolve.

Owning my courage helps me tackle the tough stuff. When I don't back away from being uncomfortable, there will be growth. Being on the other side of the "problem" feels like an accomplishment.

I don't believe we are ever given anything in life that we can't handle. It takes trust to know that diving into pain will allow the feeling of freedom to surface on the other side. From my own experience, I can say that each time I dove headfirst into feeling the pain that I faced, I came out on the other side more confident than ever. I can handle anything life has in store for me.

i'

Incurable...
No Matter What

Joe Narciso

HOW DO YOU RISE ABOVE something that is going to keep getting bigger? How do you leave something in the past that is not going to go away, no matter how hard you try to outrun it? How do you keep fighting when you know in your heart and your head that your opponent is going to get the better of you?

How do you overcome something that is not overcome-able?

I went to Fordham University to study acting. I was student body president, I founded a fraternity, and I got the mother of all internships at *Late Night with David Letterman*. So naturally, when I got out of college, I worked on Wall Street, in technology. I did pretty well there, eventually becoming the Global Head of Application Integration for one of the world's largest banks. I had staff all over the world. Things were pretty good.

On a personal level, things were great. I married my high school sweetheart and the love of my life, Charlene. We started a family—two sweet little girls. The future looked bright.

While working at the bank and enjoying a successful start to my career, the acting bug still gnawed at me. I joined the After Hours Comedy Troupe and soon got an agent. It took a while to get my first big break—as the voice of Calvin Klein Eternity. In no time, I became one of the busiest voice actors in the city. I was the voice of Olive Garden, Coca Cola, and Mercedes Benz.

Like many New York actors, I felt I could finally call myself a real professional when I got my first part on *Law & Order*. I also did *Special Victims Unit*, *The Sopranos*, *Third Watch*, and *Monk*. Life was great.

But there are moments that can radically change your path. Sometimes, they're like big, yellow detour signs. At other times, they're more like a grain of sand under your feet, hardly discernible. You might have no idea they're even there.

About five years into my acting career, I booked a major campaign for Fed-Ex, where I worked with an up-and-coming kid named Steve Carell. Call me crazy, but I still think there are big things in his future.

About this same time, I did my first Shakespeare play. As I took the stage for the first time, I began to shake like a leaf. I thought it was because I was nervous, never having done Shakespeare before. But before long, I began to shake in my auditions, on camera, on the softball field, and at home.

I didn't tell anyone, including my own family. I continued to work. I continued to play. I continued to live. But as time went by, I shook more … and I worked less. Finally, I had no choice but to admit to everyone what was now painfully obvious. I was diagnosed with Parkinson's disease.

Oddly enough, I wasn't that worried. Parkinson's is no longer something you die from—it's something you die with. I wasn't that concerned about my career, either. I figured that, as long as I could speak, I'd always be able to feed my family.

My wife Charlene could not have been more supportive. She encouraged me to leave the bank and concentrate on acting full time, despite my diagnosis. She felt, selflessly, that I would feel less stress, which would help with symptoms. But even more, she knew that if I didn't take the chance to be a full time actor now, I never would.

My two children began to notice something was wrong, too. I couldn't play with them the way I once had. I was always tired and didn't smile or laugh as often as I used to. I tried to hide my Parkinson's from them for as long as I could. I didn't want them to worry about me.

When I did finally tell them, my oldest daughter, Samantha, was upset. She wanted to know if I was dying and she didn't really believe me when I tried to assure her that I wasn't. My younger daughter, Sophia, was seemingly unmoved upon hearing the news. I assumed it was because she really didn't understand. But a few hours later, she asked, "Would it be helpful if I got a job to help pay the bills, Daddy?" This hurt more than when I was first diagnosed.

My little girls were scared, and though I wouldn't admit it, for the first time, I was scared, too. The two most innocent people in all of this were now actively worrying about me. They were unsettled about the future, anxious about not having enough money to live on—and afraid of losing me.

I had to face it. The life I had lived, the life I loved, was going to be very different from what I expected. I went from a future filled with promise, success, and limitless possibility to one of uncertainty, worry, frustration, and disability.

I have a progressively debilitating neurological disorder. Today is as good as things will ever get, physically. My condition will continue to deteriorate. So how do I overcome?

Love. I am blessed to have a wealth of great friends and a wonderful family. They are there for me whenever I need them. I have three amazing daughters (Gracie, the youngest, came along a few years ago) of whom I couldn't be more proud. And then of course, there's Charlene.

When we started dating in high school, we used to say we would always be together, no matter what. I wrote "no matter what" on every card I ever gave her. We had it engraved on our wedding rings.

So, I'll climb every hill and descend every valley, holding Charlene's steady hand. Hopefully, I won't become too big a burden to her. But I know that through it all, she will love me and I will love her. That's all the overcoming I could ever hope for … no matter what.

i

·····························

Breast Selling Author

Holly Bertone

A FEW DAYS BEFORE my thirty-ninth birthday, it dawned on me that all of the pieces of my life were finally coming together. I was living with my boyfriend, Carter, and his son (aka "Stepson"). We had recently started looking at wedding rings and were planning for the rest of our lives together.

I was ready for this new life. In the decade prior, I had bought a home, dated a lot, earned a master's degree, climbed the corporate ladder, traveled to fabulous places, raced mountain bikes, rock climbed, and drank margaritas with my girlfriends. I was happy, carefree, and in love with life. I had accomplished everything I had ever wanted to do as a single gal, and I was ready to settle down, with no regrets. I was ready to change my focus from doing my own thing to taking care of my new family.

I was excited for a new beginning. I knew going into my thirty-ninth birthday that my life would soon be changing—but I wasn't prepared for how much.

Riding home on the train on a hot August afternoon, I received a phone call from my doctor. "I'm calling with your test results. I'm sorry to let you know … you have breast cancer." Forty-eight hours later, Carter was down on one knee with the most beautiful ring. In a span of two days, my life was turned upside down by eight unforgettable words: "You have breast cancer" and "Will you marry me?" My world would never be the same again.

Most newly engaged couples pick out china patterns and decide on honeymoon destinations. I scheduled surgery. Most brides try on dresses and veils. I tried on wigs, because I would be bald on my wedding day from chemo treatment. Dinner conversations were not about whether the invitations should be white, cream, or ivory—they were about fighting cancer.

In those nine months between "Will you marry me?" and "I do," I lost part of my breast to surgery and all of my hair to treatment. I was sick from chemo, I came into early menopause, and I developed a case of the walking farts. Nothing says "beautiful and sexy fiancée" like a sweaty, bald, lopsided woman with the walking farts. And yet, Carter and Stepson never left my side.

Breast cancer typically takes away the three things that outwardly define a woman; her hair, her breasts, and her fertility—a triple threat of the worst possible kind. This kind of journey is a tough blow for any woman, and for me, these changes were impossible to accept. I was trying to be a beautiful fiancée. We tried our best to laugh through all of the changes, but I still had my share of epic-level meltdowns.

When my self-esteem hit rock bottom, I became aware that, if I felt this way, then many other women did, too. I knew this would become my calling, my purpose. I was no longer a victim.

Every bride wants to be beautiful on her wedding day. Every bride wants her wedding day to be perfect. Instead, I was the something blue. I was getting married without hair, eyebrows, or eyelashes. I was getting married with two big scars on my chest. I had fingernails that were discolored and dead, which even the best manicure couldn't fix. Chemo had taken its toll on my body.

I had to let go of the something old and embrace the something new. Beauty was not my bald head but my brains and the ability to make others laugh. Beauty was not my scars but my heart and the ability to love. Beauty was not chemical menopause but the commitment to raise my new stepson and take care of my new family.

I am a survivor.

Cancer hijacked my engagement, my wedding, and my life. At the time, it was easy to get swallowed by the "woe is me" feelings. But now, looking back at that year, I know that it was the biggest blessing I could have ever asked for.

"They" say that cancer shouldn't define you. but I disagree. Cancer defined that year for me and my family, and it set us up to be where we are today. Through the tears and heartache came a beautiful opportunity to help others and share love and inspiration with women who are hurting.

After reevaluating my "new normal" as a cancer survivor, wife, and stepmother, I made a huge decision to step down from a high-powered and demanding job. My focus changed from climbing the corporate ladder to caring for my health and my family. I walked away with no regrets.

I started blogging as a way to communicate with friends and family during and after cancer treatment. I quickly learned how much I loved writing. The Coconut Head's Survival Guide has become a forum for me to share home and family inspiration while still focusing on breast cancer advocacy and awareness. Some may brag about being a best-selling author, but after writing three books on cancer—including one for children—I can brag that I am a *breast*-selling author!

The biggest blessing has been the lives I've been able to touch through all of my outreach—and not just my fellow breast cancer survivors, but all women. We all struggle with our own self-esteem issues, our own inadequacies, and our own demons. I want to be a voice to let other women know that it's okay to love yourself. I want to help other women believe in themselves.

A wrong turn in life isn't always a bad thing. I wouldn't wish cancer on my worst enemy, but I wouldn't take it back for anything in the world.

Finding a Win in Retreat
Evita Ochel

IT WAS AN OVERCAST DAY, as I found myself standing on the edge of the beach in the northernmost tip of Oregon. It was the moment when what was to come began to fully sink in. I, along with my partner and another couple, were about to start a long-distance hike on the Oregon Coast Trail. It was my first endeavor of this type. The nature lover within me was eager and excited, but my mind couldn't help wonder with mild hesitation about the journey to come.

We began our trek that afternoon in the most pleasant of ways and had a memorable first night. Little did we know about the experiences ahead that would test our boundaries and inner balance.

The next day, we began our long walk at the break of dawn under a low, gray sky. Rain was merely moments away. As those first thick droplets fell, an interesting sensation ran through my body. In society, we are so quick to scurry for shelter at the first sign of rain—yet here we were, miles away from any kind of shelter. We marched on that day as the rain and wind pelted us from every direction. Everything was wet and cold, and we were soaked to the core.

Day Two turned into Day Three, and neither the rain nor the strong winds subsided as our trail weaved through the wide open beach, stony ridges, and dense, hilly forests.

To anyone else, the choice would have been obvious—get off the trail and take cover. But to a long-distance hiker, this kind of stuff is supposed to be part of the experience … more or less. The comfort-driven body nudged to find indoor shelter, but the purpose-driven mind didn't want to hear any of it. After all, it was only the third day of our three-week trek, and part of this experience was intended as an exercise to push beyond the comfort of personal boundaries. It would be a disappointment to duck out at the first sign of hardship. But as if the challenge of a long-distance hike wasn't enough under favorable conditions, the weather made sure that we got the most out of our experience.

In our comfort-driven culture, it may seem foolish to even have to contemplate a choice under such conditions, but anyone who has ever wanted to push their personal boundaries in any area of life can no doubt relate. There's a fine line between honoring personal needs, to maintain a healthy balance, and working with one's edge to push through personal limitations. I wanted to honor my commitment and my body, but I also wanted to honor my group's experience.

For that third night, we compromised as a group and got proper, indoor lodging. It was a wise choice, and we continued on the trail the next day. The weather calmed a bit, but I was feeling worn down by the strenuous physical experience encountered thus far. However, I was determined to keep moving forward. Then I began to feel discomfort in my left foot.

By the morning of the fifth day, the pain in my foot became more pronounced. I knew what I needed to do. I needed to get some adequate rest. Sure, I could have pushed forward, but what then? Maybe things would have gotten better, but maybe not. And what would I have proved in the end, anyway? The choice was crystal clear.

I got off the trail and took it easy for the next three days. Then, as the weather and my foot cleared up, we rejoined our group and were back on the trail again.

I cannot say that I accomplished the goal of completing that trail in full. But I learned a tremendous lesson: the importance of balancing needs and wants—knowing when to push and when to retreat. It can be so exhilarating at times to push our personal boundaries and limits, or to accomplish some goal. But there is no positive accomplishment in pushing these too far.

My trek was filled with nuggets of wisdom and personal realizations, and today I am grateful for every moment and experience I encountered.

A New Passion for Life

Julie Ryan

A T THE END OF 2005, I turned thirty. I was single (again) and had just started a new career. Three weeks later, I received a message from "the one that got away." I was happy. At age thirty, my life seemed to be starting over fresh. I had the right job. The right guy. The right life.

Fast forward to the summer of 2008. We had been married a year and a half. My dentist (along with doctors offering a second and third opinion) told me that I needed to get braces, or I'd be scheduling gum-grafting surgery for the second time in less than ten years. From Day One with the braces, I began having horrible migraines. I couldn't get off the couch and I couldn't work. I couldn't do anything except pop meds for the migraines and hope something would help. Nothing did, and eventually, all those meds gave me ulcers. Then my gallbladder went out.

This was the beginning of a never-ending list of ailments that have continued since that summer.

In 2010, I was diagnosed with fibromyalgia. By 2011, I was not only physically ill but also mentally ill. I felt like things would never get better and I was quickly losing hope that there was a future for me. I had to quit working. I was doing almost nothing except lying in bed. I was about a day away from walking into the hospital and committing myself, because I knew I was suicidal. I had not yet told my family how I was feeling. I knew I needed to, so I finally did.

I believe that finally telling my family how depressed I felt was the beginning of things turning around for me. I began seeing a psychologist and tried several different medications. We finally found one that seemed to be helping, only to discover that it shouldn't be mixed with another med I was already on. The combination landed me in the emergency room—twice. Once again, I was running out of options.

There was one thing I had not tried, one suggestion that I had ignored time and time again: diet. How could changing my diet possibly help? It didn't make sense to me. But now I was desperate and willing to try anything. I began 2012 with an elimination diet. I started with a week of nothing but juice, and followed that by slowly reintroducing food groups, with the exception of gluten, dairy, and eggs—because by the end of the juice week, my food sensitivity testing had returned, indicating that yes, I was sensitive to those foods.

I began feeling better within just a few weeks. My husband said he could see a major change in my energy level. I was even able to make a nine-hour drive to see my best friend so she could teach me how to live gluten-free. I did accidentally ingest gluten a couple of times in the next few months, and those were the only days that I felt completely fatigued and in pain. I was finally on the road to recovery.

By the summer of 2012, I had returned to living again. I was even trying CrossFit and surviving it. Heck, I wasn't just surviving it—I was loving it!

Back in 2010—when I knew I had fibromyalgia, but before I had been formally diagnosed—I began a blog detailing my journey. The idea had been to share the information I found as I found it. I was new to this illness and I knew others were, as well. They might be less likely to engage in the kind of research that I was open to doing. The blog was a way for me to both document what I found and share it with others. Over the years, my activity levels varied with the blog, but it was always there. When I began to feel better, I also began to blog a lot more.

In 2013, I was back to what I call my "new normal." I'm not 100 percent of what I used to be, but I'm at a place I can deal with. I know my limits and I know that, as long as I stay within them, I can do a lot. I can live normally. My goal was to go back to school and finish my psychology degree so that I could find additional ways of helping others deal with life. I'd never really thought about writing as a profession. Writing was just something I did.

When I was approached by Answers.com to write articles for their new Fatigue category, my first thought was that I couldn't do it. No way! However, when I told my husband about the offer, he pushed me to give it a try. I did, and I loved it. I realized that I not only enjoyed writing but that I might actually be able to make a living with it.

Chronic pain took my life away for several years, but it gave me something I never knew I had: a passion to write, and more importantly, a passion to help people through my writing. Chronic pain gave me a new life, as well as a new understanding of life, and a new appreciation for the small things and for the people in it.

I would not be the person I am today if not for the pain I've learned to live with.

Once a Cheerleader Always a Cheerleader

Barby Ingle

Y LOVE FOR DANCE, cheerleading, and gymnastics began at the age of four when I attended my first classes. I grew up a performance athlete. When I was twelve, I told my parents my dream: "I want to be a professional cheerleader." I was prepared to dedicate the rest of my life to making this come true.

"Impossible. You can't be a cheerleader the rest of your life," my father said, wagging his finger at me.

Boy, was he wrong. After college graduation, I opened up my own cheer/dance training company and was hired as head cheer dance coach at Washington State University. I was living my dream to the fullest.

Just before my thirtieth birthday, I developed a neuro-autoimmune disease called Reflex Sympathetic Dystrophy. As my world crashed around me due to my new physical limitations, I held on to hope that things would change. I had to change my focus from what I had lost to what I could still do.

Although I can no longer do amazing tricks and flips, I found another way to cheer on my team. The team changed, my coaching style had to change, and I had to rely on the emotional aspects of cheerleading instead of the physical.

Once a cheerleader, always a cheerleader. Even with Reflex Sympathetic Dystrophy (RSD) affecting every aspect of my life, my can-do cheerleading attitude shows through. Now, I advocate and cheer for all challenged with a chronic-care condition involving chronic pain as well as our families, caregivers, healthcare professionals, and the public.

This cheerleader (smile even if your team is losing) attitude has not changed through all of my pain. I still love to be with people and to be involved in volunteer activities. I have been a motivational speaker for chronic pain awareness presentations on behalf of pain patients with RSD and other neuropathy conditions since 2006, and it is very rewarding.

One in three people (116 million) in the United States are affected with a condition that causes pain, so it is bound to affect you or someone you know. But until you actually feel the pain, it is difficult to understand all of the challenges it brings on. Whether physical or mental, pain can and will consume you if you allow it to.

Only the patient can begin the process of healing. My hope is that my speaking engagements and books will inspire transformations filled with HOPE and motivation.

I am constantly doing research and I teach people about chronic pain and RSD every chance I get—even at a grocery store or on a plane. I am actively involved in various RSD and chronic pain-related events. I try to teach others so no one will have to go through the challenges I have faced because of chronic pain. I was also the inspiration for starting the Power of Pain Foundation.

Since 1997, I have been diagnosed with painful conditions ranging from reflex sympathetic dystrophy, temporomandibular joint disorder, ischemic colitis, and thoracic outlet syndrome—not to mention the particularly nasty endometriosis, which resulted in a full hysterectomy and left oophorectomy.

I know firsthand how hard it is to continue looking for relief and perfect answers, and then coming up against healthcare professionals who blow you off or do not believe what you are saying could actually be what you're experiencing. As I search for a cure, I have become my own best advocate. Now I share the information so that you can be yours.

Even after seeing more than a hundred healthcare professionals and having major surgeries I didn't need, and despite complications such as internal bleeding, medication interactions, kidney stones, tumors, severe constipation, and so much more—I did not give up or give in! I was tested to my limits and realized they are past the boundaries I had placed on myself. I had to become the Chief of Staff of my own medical team. If I can do it, anyone can.

I am actively involved in the Power of Pain Foundation, which helps low-income and underinsured patients with neuropathy pain. Through my advocacy work, I have had the pleasure of meeting thousands of patients and family members from around the country and online. Sharing my story and hearing their stories is what it's all about. From the human connection and community we create, I get my drive to advocate for myself and others.

I have done television and radio interviews to raise awareness for chronic pain and RSD in particular, using my story to motivate others. In coordination with my team of doctors, I have put videos of my procedures on YouTube and the Power of Pain Foundation's website.

I am on the front lines, connecting with people who are healthy, using my story to touch their lives and getting them to open up to accepting that, just because someone is not in a cast or brace, that does not mean that nothing is wrong with them or that they don't need assistance. Anyone can be touched by chronic pain at any time. It is what you do with what you get that makes the world a better place.

I have taken a catastrophic event and turned it into a motivation of awareness, education, and physical action. In doing so, I am carrying on my lifetime tradition of being a cheerleader. *\O/*

i'

··

Ask Me About My Colitis... No Really, Ask Me

Megan Starshak

I WAS SITTING ON THE EDGE of the stage of the Troubadour in Los Angeles, lost in the talents of Hall of Fame-caliber musicians. "How did I get here? How is this my life?" The diagnosis of an incurable digestive disease somehow had brought me to this incredible benefit concert, one of countless blessings I never imagined I would have.

In 2002, fresh out of high school and making big plans for the rest of my life, I was diagnosed with ulcerative colitis (UC). College, boyfriends, careers, adventures—none of these had included managing a life-altering disease, but as so many of us learn, life had other plans.

Crohn's disease and colitis—both inflammatory bowel diseases (IBD)—differ from patient to patient. Mine included frequent, urgent bathroom trips with loose, bloody stools. I was an empty tank of energy that no amount of sleep could refill. I had to choose between the pain of digestion or the pain of going hungry—and I often chose the latter.

Most memorably, this condition stole my identity—my brightness, my athleticism, my friends. I felt out of place among my keg-partying, road-tripping coeds, desperate for just one other person to whom I could relate. Life was spent just getting through each day, making it to classes and back home to do as little as I could with whatever I had left. Days were clouded with anger and loneliness.

The end of my college career was spent desperately waiting for the light at the end of the tunnel while trying different medicines and working to complete my degree. By May, I was ready for a change of scenery, and much needed relief—physically and socially.

My first endeavor after graduation was a three-day bicycle ride for IBD. On the first morning of that ride, I had my very first "a-ha" moment: a fellow rider turned to me and asked, "Why are you here?"

My answer at the time was, "I have colitis and I love cycling." I didn't realize the weight of that question until much later. *I am here because I was given colitis for a purpose. I was put here for a purpose, and this is the start of my journey.*

That weekend was the first time I had met other people with my disease. To hear others speak so openly about something that I had been struggling to explain or understand was profound. I was not alone. Others had been down this road before me, and they were still standing. They were happy and confident, despite having the same horrible disease as me.

Later that summer, I found myself volunteering at a weeklong IBD camp—an important stop on my newfound path of empowerment. At camp, I found a wide range of ages—from kids diagnosed as toddlers to adults with professional careers—all in different stages of life and disease, all in one place, all with IBD.

Camp is an intricate web of moments that are passed from one person to the next. Examples of strength and moments of hope come from those who have been there—people like me who have learned from those before them. This knowledge is passed on to those reaching out for the same connection and hope. It helps young patients grow with confidence and empathy beyond their years. To be a part of that process and community was an incredibly special and humbling experience.

It was at camp that I first realized the importance of taking care of yourself, wholly—finding acceptance, recognizing your own strength, and acknowledging your worth. Surrounding yourself with support, learning to put your health first, and finding your own "normal" is of the utmost important—and so is seeking out your place in the community and finding your role in the world.

At camp, everyone had IBD, and everyone knew it. But in the real world, these stories still exist, but are lost in the hustle of daily life. We needed a catalyst to bring them to the forefront.

In the weeks following camp, I was chatting with a fellow counselor about how to extend the open, fostering environment of camp. An idea hit us: Could we design a shirt that would literally get people talking? It was so simple: "Ask Me About My Colitis." We both wanted one, and we thought maybe, if we did, others would, too. This led us to what has now become our nonprofit, The Great Bowel Movement.

Everyone has a story, and so many are worth telling. Stories of IBD are filled with pain, struggle, and fear, but also with strength, pride, and wisdom. Providing tools to share them is good for the community and for the general public. It educates people while connecting faces, not medical jargon, with diseases. It shows others that you don't have to be ashamed and you don't have to hide anything.

Wearing these shirts has prompted many honest conversations. By supplying the shirts, along with online resources and a social media community, we've both found even more purpose and opportunity in our diagnoses than we ever dreamed.

Connecting with others—whether it leads me to an incredible concert, a bike ride, a camp for kids, or an online community—is one of the best parts of my own experience. When I first heard my diagnosis, all those years ago, I would have never imagined my life to be as purposeful and fulfilling as it is today, and I definitely wouldn't have thought colitis would be the reason for it all.

My pre-college, pre-diagnosis plans for life have changed, but my career, my relationships, and my adventures are greater than I could have ever dreamed.

i'

Trauma

"TRAUMA IS PERSONAL. It does not disappear if it is not validated."
- Danielle Bernock

i

We All Need Cleaner Fish

Suzanne Paire

FASCINATING FACT: deep in our vast oceans, batfish line up for a good cleaning. It's a car wash of sorts—like a shower with an S.O.S.® soap pad. They have parasites and they need them gone—off, swallowed up immediately. The parasites are undetectable by the human eye, but if left to feast, they will bring sores, fungus, and for most fish, death.

As I get older and see more, read more, and get acquainted with more people, it is clear that many of us live with our own parasitic, life-sucking leeches. I don't mean the relative or friend that never seems to have their wallet. I mean the matters of the mind and heart—the injuries and traumas laid on us by cruel, selfish, or broken people. When such a scar is left unattended, left to build a carbon-sustained life of its own, it can breed in ways often naked to the human eye … and these scars can kill.

{ 79 }

I'm referring to the "stuff" that festers, making an individual angry, bitter, and suspicious. Or the junk that makes us settle for an unfulfilling life, setting aside or never picking up our goals and dreams of furthering our education, or that makes us avoid asking that special someone out on a date or shy away from reaching for that promotion.

It could be the belief that we are unlovable, expendable, dumb, ugly, or easily forgotten. Whatever it is, it needs attention because, subtle or not, such a belief may be subtracting from your joy and happiness, eating away at your outlook, and putting a fungus on your success.

I was twenty-one, aiming for purity and trusting. I was innocent but not dumb. Sadly, my father's long-time friend, who was fifty-five years old at the time, was neither smart nor innocent.

It was up to me the night my parents were out of town to keep my clothes on and get out of the house as a virgin, the way I had entered. It was up to me to push away the experienced, groping hands that wanted and aimed to take everything that I worked to preserve for someone I deemed deserving. It was up to me to comprehend the surprise of a friend becoming an enemy in a matter of seconds … and to somehow forget his touch.

I did keep my clothes on with effort that night, defeating my paralyzing fear. I did get back home. And I did curl up in a ball in my bed, tucked tight against the wall, sobbing, wondering, "Will my parents believe me? How do I navigate this mess?" And knowing: "This will break my father's heart."

Before I fell asleep that night, I chose anger to replace the sadness and fear. It felt stronger, and it was easy to loathe becoming a statistic.

Within forty-eight hours, I also discovered something else that I hated: my mother's "bury it" method of coping. She had good intentions, but her continued friendship with this man and keeping this scenario a secret from my father was arguably more damaging than the event itself. Exactly how many birthday dinners, holiday parties, and weekly visits was I to endure in the name of keeping the peace? His invitation to my wedding five years later, at the dismissal of some of my dear college friends, was the breaking point for sure.

It is important to know that the sea bears traitors as well. *Aspidontus rhinorhynchos* is one example of a fish that poses as a cleaner fish, breaking the literal "truce contract" shared for a few seconds or minutes between a host and a cleaner fish—who, under other circumstances, would be predator and prey. After the host requests a cleaning through body language, his defenses are down and he is vulnerable to attack. It is then that the *Aspidontus rhinorhynchos* bites him, taking a piece of his body as a meal.

We meet these individuals in life—those who use and abuse, pretending to be someone they are not, hiding their malignant desire to consume a piece of us for their own edification. It is our job to *not* quit life after they succeed.

It took five years for me to realize I needed freedom and a good scrubbing to scrape off disease-causing parasites that had found, in spite of my efforts, steady lodging in my mind and heart. I discovered a great counselor who acted as my Wrasse cleaner fish.

"Oh, I'm not weak for having needs and struggling with trust?"

"It wasn't my fault *at all*?"

"I'm not tarnished?"

"It's not disrespectful to acknowledge that my mother handled this poorly … and I can tell her that?"

"Someone can love you *and* betray you?"

"I am not alone?"

"I am allowed to tell my folks I won't attend that holiday party if he's there?"

"I can set boundaries?"

Forgiveness does cost. I knew I would pay that price in this scenario. But, I also knew I would pay a bigger price if I let all of this perpetually burn inside, changing my opinion of myself and my outlook on the world.

Parasites went down the drain with the right cleaning and maintenance, and my thought-life changed. My head cleared and my soul breathed new energy. I had a better understanding of how my mother could act in a way that spoke of betrayal by protecting the man who betrayed my father and me at the deepest level. I had new understanding and empathy, and thus the ability to forgive my father, who tossed blaming words my way once he was told.

With my walls and coping mechanisms down—or at least understood—I felt a new lease on life. It changed my relationships, including mine with myself. I had wisdom, understanding, tenderness, forgiveness, humility, and freedom. Parasites still come, and cleanings are still needed. I continue the work of living "Arms Open Wide," head sponged, washing away any fungus that might blur my vision or stifle my success.

i

....

An Uncommon
Compassion
Jane Beller

PICTURE THIS. You spend an enormous amount of time inventing worst-case scenarios in your mind, worthy of the most ridiculous soap opera story lines. You are irrationally fearful of becoming homeless. You jump at loud noises. You have the most frightening nightmares several times a week. The term "day-mares" seems absurd to most people, but not to you; you laugh because you understand exactly what it means. You have this voice in your head telling you, several times a day, that you should "just kill yourself." It speaks as if suicide is the simplest solution to even the most banal problem.

I lived that way for twenty years. Then one day, I was called upon to report for jury duty. I couldn't look toward one side of the courtroom. I was shaking violently. I was terrified. When they tried to calm me down by saying I might not have to serve in this actual courtroom but "down that hall, where that door is," I looked down the empty hallway and screamed. Something was terribly wrong. I stumbled out of there, crying, and then called my sister and told her I was crazy.

Rewind, twenty years earlier. I was fifteen and my sister was nineteen, and we were abducted by a man. He posed as a policeman. He took us in his car to a dark street. He held a knife to my back, pushed my face into the car radio, and sexually molested my sister, with me in between them. He told us repeatedly that he was doing this for our own good. That there are bad people out there. That he was doing us a favor.

The cops knew who it was the minute we called them. He was not a first-time offender, but they had never successfully prosecuted him. Five months later, we were in a courtroom. The defense attorney tried to accuse us of being prostitutes. Our kidnapper was a few feet away, staring me down, unblinking, like Charles Manson. The defense attorney kept badgering me, asking me how many fingers the man put into my sister's vagina. I was still a child. I was virgin. I felt as if all the grown-ups in the room had abandoned me.

We put him in jail on two counts of kidnapping, one count of assault with a deadly weapon, and one count of sexual assault. I do not regret putting him in jail. I never have. I couldn't have lived thinking he would do this to anyone else. But the court case took its toll on me.

Fast-forward to mandatory jury duty, many years later. Somehow, I turned into that traumatized fifteen-year old girl and my kidnapper was staring me down from the side of the courtroom. Afterwards, I went to see a therapist, and he said, "Well, you know you have PTSD, right?" Clearly, I didn't. I had seen many a therapist before, but PTSD had never been mentioned. It wasn't a known entity yet.

PTSD is Post Traumatic Stress Disorder. It is a mental health condition resulting from a traumatic event. Humans are born with an innate need to avoid or defend themselves from danger, and we all have natural flight, fight, and freeze responses. It is normal to feel fear when you are in these situations. But people like me feel fear when there is no danger.

A trigger is the catalyst that brings on these reactions. It could be something as simple as a song, or a scene in a film, or a television program. It could be a news event, a loud noise, or a person's emotional outburst.

When I am triggered, I become dazed and feel like a deer in the headlights. That is my "freeze" response. Or I can get speedy and jumpy, and sometimes I impulsively remove myself from an uncomfortable situation. Those are my "flight" responses. I feel the need to physically defend people when I perceive a danger. That is my "fight" response.

Not knowing I was triggered all those years, and unaware of what PTSD was, I did not realize I could find help.

I found the right therapist for me. Simply put, she makes me feel better. I work very hard in therapy, and I leave her office every time with a renewed pep in my step. I have actually skipped down the city street after leaving her office. That skip is her doing. She helps return me to the same funny child I once was.

Talk therapy and EMDR (Eye Movement Desensitization & Reprocessing Therapy*) are tools that have changed my life. And I get to do them with probably the kindest soul I've ever met. I am learning how to understand PTSD and live peacefully with it.

I don't have to pretend to be brave and act tough all the time. I can just be me. I am not frightened as often. I have learned to recognize signs of my PTSD, and I now have tools to gently pull myself back in off the proverbial ledge.

They say that PTSD never goes away. But instead of it being a living nightmare, it has just become a part of me that I must consistently tend to and look after. I now more naturally select friends who are empathetic and understanding and who choose positive paths around their own roadblocks.

My situation has actually given me a gift: not only can I empathize with others' struggles, but I can offer them a sort of uncommon compassion. That is the silver lining to my dark cloud. I can show up and bring them a small ray of sunshine.

* For more information about PTSD Peter Levine's books are highly recommended.
* For more information about EMDR and/or to find a trained therapist, go to: http://www.emdr.com

i'

Coming to Terms

Dana Kukin

N THE MIDDLE of my sophomore year at Barnard College, I attended a documentary screening at the annual Athena Film Festival. The film, *Brave Miss World*, tells the story of Linor Abargil, an Israeli model who was crowned Miss World in 1998. Seven weeks before receiving this title, Linor was raped by a travel agent in Milan. The documentary chronicles Linor's battle to serve justice to her attacker, and the subsequent work she began to help other survivors. I was incredibly moved by Linor's strength and bravery. Little did I know that soon, this film would save my life.

Three months later, I was raped and beaten by a stranger in a city far from home. I was twenty years old. Physically, he was much stronger than I was, and after he had pinned me down, I had no ability to fight him off. He told me he wouldn't harm my face because he thought I was beautiful. But he pummeled me and left my body covered in scratches and bruises.

It took me several days before I could even utter the word "rape," and it was months before I was able to recall certain details that my mind had blocked out.

I didn't tell anyone about what happened, but my immediate thoughts turned to the film I had seen a few months before. While I was scared and shaken, I was quick to understand that I was a survivor, not a victim—and that I was not alone. The film gave me the courage and conviction to move forward.

I did finally confide in a few people, including my brother and a doctor. I thought the worst was behind me, but I was not prepared for the long road ahead. I didn't tell my parents or my sister for a long time. Often, it's more difficult to share terrible news with those you love the most.

I tried to push the incident out of my mind and just move on—but soon enough, I began to display symptoms of PTSD. Nightmares, flashbacks, and panic attacks haunted me. My brother was the only person who consistently checked in on me. I told some friends, and I suspect a few of them were afraid to talk to me about what had happened. Most friends I had told were very supportive … yet none of them knew how to help me.

Even my psychiatrist failed to follow through. When we finally scheduled a visit, two months after the rape, she forgot and missed the appointment. I tried seeking out support groups in New York, but was unsuccessful. Every lead resulted in a dead end. When I found a support group at a hospital, they denied me entry because of their rule that members could join only up to six months after the assault. They simply emailed me to advise I would not be welcome. They offered an individual meeting, but since I was already shut out of the group, I wasn't interested.

I reached out to my school's counseling center at the beginning of the fall semester. They were kind and promised to help me find a group. They sent one follow-up email, but then I never heard from them again. About a month later, I had a particularly crippling panic attack in my dorm room. My roommate called Health Services, but they told her since it was Sunday evening, I had to go to an emergency room. I went back to the counseling center later that week, and this time they gave me the phone number of a clinic in Manhattan. I called to make an appointment, but because I was not suicidal, the earliest time slot they could offer me was more than a month later. I knew I would not last that long.

With the help of my parents, in whom I finally confided, and my roommate, I found a private therapist. We worked together through intensive therapy, often meeting three times a week. During this time, I was carrying a full load of courses, working in an internship off-campus, and serving as an active member of committees for both Barnard College and the Columbia/Barnard Hillel.

During the summer, I met with the Hillel rabbi and told him what had happened to me. I asked him to help me create a program in school relating to mental health awareness. I needed to channel my energy into making something positive evolve from this horror—to make sense of something so senseless.

That was the day the Columbia/Barnard Hillel's Mental Health Awareness Month was born. I emailed Cecelia Peck, the director of *Brave Miss World*, and told her my story. She responded within twenty minutes, giving me the confidence boost I needed. We screened her film on Wednesday, November 20, 2013. Watching Linor on screen again emboldened me to address the audience after the film and describe what had happened to me. This was the first time I'd spoken publicly about the incident.

The decision to write for *The i'Mpossible Project* was not an easy one, but it has been an important part of my healing process. It's daunting to imagine the many people who will read this and learn what happened to me: extended family, close friends, ex-boyfriends, even strangers. But I do not feel shame for what happened, and telling my story is part of the feeling of empowerment and control that I now crave.

Rape can happen to anyone. My goal is to give hope and encouragement to other survivors of rape, so they understand that they should not be afraid to ask for help nor get discouraged if they reach some dead ends.

It has been a little over a year since I was raped. Some days are worse than others, but I grow more confident each day. I've reached a level of clarity that I never thought I could. What I experienced was horrible, but I am turning this trauma into a catalyst for change. I hope my story and my actions can help someone the way Linor's story helped me.

i'

Staying Tuned to the Brightside

Jenny Rietveld

ON THE 25TH OF JULY, 2011, I had a nightmare that my son Gary was running on a bridge. He was scared and screaming that someone was after him. I instantly awoke, frightened and sweating. I happened to be on holiday in the United States, away from my home and native land (Oh! Canada), and would be returning later that day. In the morning, I confided in several members of my family about the awful dream I'd had about Gary.

At 8:30pm that same night, we got a call from my son's friend in Vancouver. He told us that two joggers had found Gary in Stanley Park near the Lions Gate Bridge at 7 a.m.—dead. In shock and disbelief, we immediately phoned the police department in Vancouver. "Yes it's true," they said, with no sign of compassion. His time of death had been approximated at 4 a.m. They told us it would be a few days before they could release his body.

We went ahead and made plans to have a service for him and then bring him home. Soon after, we got another call from the police department telling us that they needed more time because they had found marks on his neck. They would now have a detective investigating my son's death. His apartment was locked up while they looked for clues. We had to put arrangements for his service on hold.

We then got another call from the police department saying they had released his body to his friend. This friend had not lived with our son for the last two-and-a-half years. How could they do this? In no time, the police flip-flopped and said we could go to Gary's apartment and take what we wanted. But we were not to let anyone in—not even the friend who had his body. We were allowed to take Gary's personal effects, but had no right to his body? Something wasn't adding up.

When we got the report back from the police, it said "cause of death unknown," but they did not close the case. All kinds of thoughts went through my head. Was Gary murdered? Was he the victim of gay bashing? Did he take his own life? What is being covered up? I eventually went into a state of shock and fell into a depression. I did not want to see anyone. I retreated into myself.

One day in the fall of 2011, I was on the internet and something caught my eye. It was a radio program called The Bright Side Show. They had a guest coming up, Suzy Ward, author of *Matthew, Tell Me about Heaven*, which was about conversations with her deceased son. I knew I had to listen to that show. I wanted to make contact with my son Gary.

Suzy spoke about her conversations with her dead son, Matthew, and shared many of the things they discussed and the questions she had asked him about the afterlife. That show helped me to see that perhaps death is not so final, after all. I felt a bit better, and I started to communicate with the host of The Bright Side Show, David, on a regular basis. He listened and tried to help me get through my depression by suggesting books I should read and supportive people with whom I should connect.

I was now a regular listener to The Bright Side Show. Another guest David interviewed was a guy named Josh, who talked about suicide prevention and depression—two cold mistresses to whom I could relate. I still hadn't quite found my will to live. I also kept thinking that my son's death wasn't foul play and that maybe he had jumped off the Lions Gate Bridge.

I thought back to whether I had seen Gary show any of the suicidal signs that Josh talked about during his interview with David. I didn't remember seeing any, but I admired the work Josh did for suicide prevention, and I really enjoyed that show. I checked out his website, and we became friends on Facebook.

One day, while talking with David, I found out that Josh was coming to a university in my hometown to perform his one-man show, *Kicking My Blue Genes in The Butt*. Perhaps he would be my guest ... and he agreed. My husband and I picked him up at the airport and I felt honored to meet him and become his friend. I got to see him perform and we shared some wonderful talks.

We never received any real answers about our son's death. We are still checking into this. We have never seen his remains, and the case still hasn't been closed. We don't really know where he is or what really happened that night. But I handle it better these days, thanks to new friendships and new ways of looking at life.

I may not have talked to my dead son, but I have felt his presence through both Josh and David. For that, I am very grateful. I'm staying tuned to the bright side. That is good news.

i

....

The Scars That Leave a Roadmap

Rachel Brummert

THEY SAY THAT YOU NEVER KNOW how strong you are until being strong is the only choice you have. In 2006, at the age of thirty-six, my life would be irreparably altered—and being "strong" was the only choice I had.

Sitting in the exam room at my primary physician's office, I was feeling miserable. I had a bad headache, I was congested, and my face felt like it was filled with concrete. I was looking forward to going home after I picked up my antibiotic. I couldn't wait to climb into bed and camp out under the covers until I felt better.

When I filled the prescription, I was not warned of the severe adverse reactions associated with the antibiotic.

A few days after finishing the medication, I was feeling a lot better. Dark, angry storm clouds obliterated the midday sun, and I wanted to run some errands before it started to rain. This was my last stop, only two blocks from home.

As I walked across the parking lot to my car, I felt something and heard it at the same time—a loud snap and searing pain. My foot gave out and I fell to the ground, scraping my hands in an attempt to break my fall.

At the hospital, it was discovered that I had ruptured my Achilles tendon in my right foot and it had balled up in my calf.

As I was recovering from that rupture, I ruptured the Achilles tendon in my other foot. I was barely able to walk because I lost the use of my left foot and was still recovering from the injury to my right foot.

A few months later, the Achilles tendon in my left foot ruptured again, this time above the original rupture. Because the tendon had ruptured twice, it couldn't be repaired by the usual procedure of sewing it back together. My ankle needed a total reconstruction. My surgeon had to take another tendon out of my foot and move it to where my Achilles should be. He had to move muscles around and then drill an anchor into my heel bone to secure the new tendon. To this day, I still have bone pain, and I have had to adjust how I walk to keep my balance.

The third rupture baffled my surgeon and me—it was practically unheard of for anyone to have three ruptures within a year and a half. We decided to go over my medical history in more detail to try to find a cause. As an afterthought, I mentioned that, aside from a sinus infection in 2006, I had not had any health problems.

"What were you prescribed for the sinus infection?" he asked.

It took me a few seconds to remember. "Levaquin," I said.

He stopped writing in my chart and put his pen down as a grave look colored his face. "You may not know this," he said, leaning on the exam table. "Levaquin is associated with serious adverse reactions, including, but not limited to, tendon ruptures."

I had a hard time accepting that someone could suffer adverse reactions long after stopping a medication, but when I went home, I researched it. I was shocked that a few pills that are supposed to help someone feel better could disable an otherwise healthy person.

I went on to rupture tendons in my right wrist, right elbow, left thumb, left ring finger, both knees, and the back of my right tibia—ten ruptures in all. Each injury required reconstructive surgery and years of grueling, painful physical therapy.

In addition to the tendon ruptures, I have permanent nerve damage, joint pain, muscle wasting, chronic widespread pain, and spinal disc degeneration—for which I have plates and screws in my spine.

The most serious adverse reaction that I have suffered was when I was diagnosed with a progressive form of a neurodegenerative disease. Because of this disease, my doctors predict that a time will come when I cannot take care of myself and I will have to rely on my loved ones to help me with even the most basic of human needs. I also lost most of my short-term memory, and my long-term memory is progressively fading away. Friends and family show me photos of people and places I should know, but I have no recollection of the person or event. My motor and cognitive function will continue to decline until it steals my last breath.

My life changed dramatically because I took an antibiotic that was inappropriately prescribed, and I was never warned of the adverse reactions associated with the medication. In fact, it turned out that I'd never had a sinus infection in the first place. The medical bills and loss of income led to financial hardships, and it took a physical and emotional toll on me and my family.

I threw my anger and frustration into action by warning others so this never happens to them. I could not and do not dwell on what I cannot do anymore because I am disabled. I have learned to accept help and to appreciate the things I can still do, because those things are so precious to me.

With an excellent support system and a passion for my work, I am no longer ashamed about my scars. I do not let them define me. Scars show us where we have been—they do not dictate where we are going.

Breaking the Cycle, Renewing the Soul

Bob Brader

I HAVE TO ADMIT, THE IDEA of taking a spin class had never appealed to me. I was looking for a good cardio workout and never thought that I would get it from just riding a stationary bike. But with all the raves SoulCycle was getting from everyone I talked to about it, I decided to give it a try.

I was shown to my bike and taught how to set it up, and I proceeded to snap my rented shoes onto the pedals. The instructor was putting us through all sorts of core-building exercises like push-ups on the handlebars and crunches while she yelled out encouraging statements. "Go at your own pace." "You are here for you." "Live your life like you ride your bike." We also had some time when we were just riding, and during that time, my mind drifted back to my old bike.

I hadn't thought about that bike in a long time. It was a yellow five-speed with a black banana seat and huge handlebars that made me feel like I was riding a motorcycle. I had attached a small radio in between the handlebars with a lot of tape. I had also attached a long, thin orange pole to the back of the bike, with a flag that had the Road Runner on it. I loved that bike.

After that first SoulCycle class, I was smiling, just thinking about riding around the back streets of Whitehall, Pennsylvania. It had been a pretty fierce workout, and I decided to do it again. The more I went to SoulCycle, the more I pushed myself, trying to get as much out of the workout as I could. I was enjoying the intensity of it.

During one class a few weeks ago, I was riding very hard, and the instructor was calling out some of those encouraging things, only this time she said: "Forget about everything outside this room; no one can hurt you while you are on your bike."

With that, I was no longer in this room; I was that little boy riding my bike as hard and as fast as I could. I was riding through the pain of having an abusive father, riding through the fear of getting hit again, tearing through the streets, working though the anger and depression, many times having to pedal standing because of the bruises on my behind and my legs.

This was my release, this was my escape, and she was right: no one could hurt me while I was riding my bike—this was my freedom. While I was on that bike, I could work out all of those pent-up emotions and truly feel alive. I was not just riding to get away from him; I was riding to overcome him.

When my mind finally brought me back to the class, I realized I was crying. Thankfully, nobody noticed, because I sweat like crazy during these classes. However, I was not sad. These were tears of joy.

When I used to look back on my childhood, I would often feel sorry for that little boy. Now I realized how resourceful he was. He could have turned that anger and bitterness against other people, or turned it on himself. Instead, he chose to ride it off on his bike, the bike he loves, the bike that made him feel free.

i'

....

Mental Health

"DO NOT CONFUSE my bad days as a sign of weakness. Those are actually the days I am fighting my hardest."
- Unknown

The Secret
Depression Club
Mae L'Heureux

TIME IS AN ODD THING, isn't it? One day we're eight, wide-eyed and optimistic, and then suddenly we are eighteen, sitting in a college dorm room, so depressed we're not sure if we'll survive the night. How does that happen? How do little girls and boys go from happy-go-lucky spirits to sad, lonely, traumatized souls? I wish I knew. I so wish I knew.

I have depression. And anxiety. My whole pretty world was turned upside down in my freshman year of college. I had always thought anxiety was my primary problem, but the dark wave of depression came over me in January 2011, as I was beginning my second semester.

Until then, I had never really heard of depression. My life was consumed with social phobia, counting rituals, and the skin-crawling feeling that every person with severe anxiety experiences. It was what I was used to. I could handle it. I would even go as far to say that anxiety was my friend.

Depression wasn't in my vocabulary—and even if it was, I knew it couldn't happen to me. But it could, and it did, and I had no idea how to respond to it. It counter-acted my anxiety, which was everything I knew. I was comfortable with anxiety until depression came in like a bulldozer and tore me apart at my core. It ripped off my security blanket and left me raw and vulnerable. It was clear to me that the anxiety and depression weren't going to coexist, so I had to make room for depression, because it wasn't going anywhere.

It started slowly. I was sleeping a lot more than usual, but not enough to cause significant alarm. Then it turned into skipping meals, and social activities, and studying. I did not care about a thing. Then the disease picked up speed and there was no turning back—I was the textbook definition of major depression, although I tried to fight that label with the little amount of energy I had left.

Looking back on it now, I kick myself for not reaching out sooner. But when you're in it, when you're trying to swim away from the monster but end up only kicking in place, you can't get help. You can barely lift a finger, let alone begin to think that telling someone might be a good idea.

After relentlessly arguing with my roommate and friends, I decided it was time to end this and get help. I went to counseling, but it sucked and made me feel worse. My roommate so badly wanted to tell someone who could help, but I'd made her swear that she wouldn't, because I was so afraid of what would happen to me if an administrator discovered how bad a state I was in. I wasn't prepared for this to happen, so I didn't know what the consequences would be.

After some scary nights and many terrifying moments, the semester was over and I was free. We kept the secret. I was still alive, and no one except my roommate and I knew how bad it was. It was like a secret depression club that we would forever belong to.

That summer, the story emerged, and my parents made me go to therapy. I think, deep down, I knew the fight wasn't over, but I pretended everything was okay because I did not want college to be taken away from me. I had too much to lose. At the time, I didn't realize it was my life that I was fighting for.

Through the grace of God, a loving family, supportive friends, and helpful mentors, I got through it. I don't say I beat depression, because I didn't. It's a disease, and I got through one episode of it, and it took three years.

There are days when getting out of bed is nearly impossible. There are meals that I still don't eat because I feel fat. There are moments when I don't want to participate in life because I feel worthless. But instead of getting overwhelmed and scared when those dark thoughts come back, I take care of myself.

I have to be in tune with how I'm feeling and now I know exactly what to do when life starts feeling like too much. People will say that I'm so strong for getting through this, but I know that I survived that horrific time in my life because people cared about me when I didn't care about myself.

My experiences with mental illness were not something I appreciated until after I got through the worst of it. As I reflect on the past four years of my life, I am overcome with nothing but joy. Anxiety and depression taught me hope, love, and service. My ordeal strengthened my relationship with God and my bonds with family and friends. It showed me what matters in life—and for that, I will be forever grateful.

Because of everything that happened, I better understand just how precious life really is. It's fragile and can be ripped away from any of us in an instant. But we don't live that way. We think we're invincible and that pain, suffering, and heartbreak can't touch us.

The best way to use our God-given gifts is to approach each day with hope, love, and the faith that He is bigger than anything trying to bring us down. When the clock strikes twelve each night, we're given a fresh start. The goal of this life is to be better than we were the day before.

My challenge for myself, and you, is to not accept mediocrity. You are strong and worthy. Keep fighting.

i

....

Passover and Possibilities

Efrem Epstein

'LL BE HONEST, WHEN I FIRST started to draft my "i'Mpossible sto-ry," I thought of the natural tie-in to Passover—and it caused me a great deal of angst. But why? This should be such an easy piece for me to write. The organization I founded, Elijah's Journey, ties so natu-rally into Passover. In fact, we've even drafted a piece for Jews around the globe to read when opening the door for Elijah at their Se-der, giving them an opportunity to spread awareness on the issue of suicide awareness and prevention on this special night.

Ultimately, it dawned on me why this task was so difficult. I had told the same story so many times that it was no longer simple to make it fresh. Every angle relating Elijah's Journey to Passover had already been used. Every angle ... but one.

On Passover night, we are supposed to relive the story as if we had exited slavery ourselves. In 2006, I was in the midst of one of the toughest emotional battles of my life, fighting what was, in many ways, my own personal Pharaoh.

Depression can parallel enslavement in many ways. Like the Children of Israel, I also tasted the bitterness and tears that are respectively symbolized by the Maror (herbs) and saltwater on the Seder table. I also can relate to how the Israelites cried out with the hope that someone, perhaps G-d, would be listening (Exodus 2:23-24).

I was lucky enough to see my own personal Exodus on July 14, 2006, the day that I was blessed to emerge from depression. However, the Bible does not end with Exodus 12, and neither did my journey.

I'm not sure I really had my Red Sea-crossing experience until a few months later, when I decided to start talking publicly about my struggles. How would people react? Would they remain silent out of fear of saying the wrong thing? Would I ever be dateable again? How could I be confident that future invitations were real acts of friendship and not simply acts of pity?

To my surprise, the most common response was for someone to, in turn, confide in me about their own struggles and/or the struggles of someone close to their heart. There was something comforting in learning that I wasn't quite the aberration that I assumed myself to be. However, there was also something very disturbing in learning that so many others were suffering silently, alone and in fear.

It took a mere six weeks for the Jews leaving Egypt to arrive at Sinai (Exodus 19:1). For me, it took much longer.

On the morning of September 10, 2009, I arrived at the base of a giant, man-made mountain range on the banks of the East River, otherwise known as The United Nations Headquarters. It was World Suicide Prevention Day, and the theme that year was "Suicide Prevention in Different Cultures." One amazing presentation followed another, outlining how suicide awareness/prevention programming and messaging can effectively be maximized by recognizing and working with the special nuances and attributes of a community. By the end of the day, the vision of an organization focused on suicide awareness/prevention in the Jewish community was in play, and by the end of the year, it had a name: Elijah's Journey.

Like the Passover narrative, my story has a mostly happy ending. But mixed with that joy are several important lessons. Nobody is immune to emotional battles and, as noted on Seder Night in the V'Hi Sheamdah prayer, peaceful times in the present are no guarantees that the future will always be calm.

Several people far better and stronger than I were not as lucky as I and, on many levels, it is important for me to spill drops from my wine glass as I work to make our imperfect world one that is a better and safer place for both me and others.

Perhaps most of all the lesson of Passover is that anything is possible. Yes, anything is possible—and i'Mpossible, too.

i'

Overcoming Anxiety and Reclaiming My Power

Audrey Dimola

THERE COMES A MOMENT in life when one realizes, "Hey, I don't have to feel this way." It's liberating, scary, and exhilarating ... because suddenly, you know that life doesn't just "happen." It's up to you how you react—your perspective, your emotions, your perception.

In the wake of a new year, as the calendar turned to 2014, I came to a point when I, too, realized, "Hey, I don't have to feel this way."

When people meet me, they immediately peg me as a firecracker of high energy and positivity—a glass-half-full (or overflowing) type of person. This has always been the core of who I am. But recently, I had lost that part of myself.

I've always struggled with anxiety, and in recent years, it had wrecked me. I seized the day until there was nothing left for seizing. I wanted so much to live every moment that I fixated obsessively on everything: love, time, regrets, and dying. It left me feeling completely disconnected from my body. I became so distrustful of my physical and mental situation that I even became too scared to ride elevators or subways (and I am a born and bred New Yorker).

I was a limitless person who felt constantly bound by limits. Butting up against what I wanted to do, but felt I couldn't do, was paralyzing. At times, the nearly ever-present anxiety faded into complete emptiness that somehow, in comparison, felt even worse. I had "rat in a cage" syndrome—knee-jerk reactions, restlessness, extreme high and low emotions, and the bottomless sense of disappointment that came from realizing that I did know better, yet I couldn't find a way to make it all work.

When does this moment of clarity arrive, and why? I can't even pinpoint it. There just comes a time of recognition, after wrestling with advice from friends and family and fighting against yourself. The small victories that add up, the resonance of deep inherent truths, the glimmering appreciation of the simple things that give you joy—you know that these are all signs from the universe saying, "Hey, you are not lost yet. It's not too late for you." It's a shift in perspective. And no one can make that shift except for you.

One day I realized, I don't want this friction in my life. And instead of stewing in it, ruminating on it, beating myself up, and slamming against the walls, I would roll with it. Twist with it. Whichever way it went, I would make it work.

Thinking of it in that way is what made it make sense. Instead of running headlong with the fear and following it into the darkness, instead of putting all my trust in the self-deprecation, stress, insecurity, and anxiety that had become so familiar—I made a conscious effort to tell myself to dig. My metaphorical shovel helped me unearth answers to questions like, "Where is this feeling coming from?" and "Is this fear legitimate or unfounded?"

I'm more than a year out from my epiphany, and I almost can't recognize the new waters I'm navigating. My heart has broken open and I am riding the current of the universe in a way I never have before. In those moments when I feel I've lost it all, when it seems pointless and I'm tired of struggling—when I feel trapped, angry, and isolated—I remind myself: "Let go. Don't fixate. This is not the end. There is always more." These thoughts put me back on track to swirl freely with this gorgeous, mad dance of life instead of focusing so hard on remembering the steps.

Here I am, not living in the past, present, or future, but in total abundance. I'm beginning an incredible journey of love, performing and sharing my artistic work, curating shows and bringing people together, receiving new opportunities. I'm staying wild and staying grateful. I'm not afraid anymore of unfulfilled potential. I don't have to wait for things to happen to me. I'm making things happen.

Sometimes all we need to do is breathe and remind ourselves that we truly are limitless. We can remember that there is more to us than the stress, the job, the rent, the endless noise, the list of demands, the weight of our ambition. We are connected to something greater, something that is blessing us each second we are alive.

At every moment, there is a new opportunity to look at ourselves and ask, "What can I do to eliminate the friction in my life? Is it perceived? Am I creating it? Am I victimizing myself? Am I perpetuating circumstances that make me uncomfortable or are holding me back? Am I surrounding myself with people who love and support me? Or am I just beating my head against the wall?"

Make a commitment to yourself to look at the signs all around you. Look for past patterns in your life—explanations of perceived coincidences—that will help you make sense of the waters that lie ahead. True bravery is looking inside yourself to examine the dreams untapped, the spirit boundless, the fire within waiting to ignite.

Move with passion, with boldness, with grace, and with uncompromising exuberance toward the things you love.

Now is the moment ... to make your own luck.

The Lessons of War

Jenny Pacanowski

THE LESSONS OF WAR, I BELIEVE, are different for everyone.

Often, I have heard that war/conflict stays with you, seeps into your soul, creates mortal injury—a restlessness that is irresolvable even with time.

Post-Traumatic Stress Disorder (PTSD) is not curable.

Creating discourse between what I believed to be true before the War, and the truth I have lived with every day after the War:

We bring the war home with us.

My lesson is, even though the War is a part of us,

It does not have to define who we are as veterans, as people, or as beings in this universe.

It will, however, affect our perceptions.

Ever since my return from Iraq, I have felt that my experiences in War have controlled and conquered who I was, how I react to other people, how I view myself, and what my future would be.

From 2005 to 2011, I was a victim and prisoner to my emotions, my PTSD, my co-dependent relationships, and my addictions. Slowly,

I dealt with my outbursts of anger instead applying the sledgehammer of rage to ALL situations. I started with a mallet of discussing what I was angry about and not just destroying everything in my path. My rage was fueled by my pain and grief over what I had lost.

My Idealism

Of love

Of friendship

Of family

Of humanity

Of the value of life.

But in 2007, my will to live was waning. In an effort to avoid the VA psychiatric hospital, I made my mother a promise that if I decided on the method, time, and place of my suicide, I would call her before taking action. However, this safety net would only save me from killing myself and would not actually help me live.

One day, my mother's friend Andrea asked if fostering a shelter dog might help me. The moment I started fostering and training bullmastiffs, I had a reason to wake up. The dog needed to be fed, to go outside, and to be loved. In 2008, I was invited to a veterans' retreat. At the last moment, I refused to drive because of the fear that I would flashback to convoying on the roads of Iraq. My mother stepped in and drove me from Pennsylvania to Martha's Vineyard. This was my first experience in a community of veterans talking, understanding each other, writing, and creating combat paper—a project in which old military uniforms are made into sheets of paper that are then used for artwork by veterans.

As the years passed, I allowed myself to grieve the loss of my idealism. My youth had been replaced with a hatred and resentment for everything I thought this country once stood for: honor, integrity, leadership, selfless service, loyalty, a fearless solidarity, and defense for what is right. Soberly, I grieved and cried for my betrayed youth and released the pain, feeling not weak, but empowered.

Since then, I have discovered an internal map to guide me. It started with throwing away the VA meds, the bottles of whiskey and vodka. I put the needle down and ended the guilt of using my extensive medical knowledge to get high, escape, and be numb.

To finally walk away from my hope of death and trailblaze a new path of not only learning for myself how to transition from war and the military culture but help others in their journey back.

I moved to Ithaca, New York to expand my comfort zone and embrace the future I never thought I would live long enough to see. I began working with the Veterans' Sanctuary, a nonprofit organization that provides a holistic approach and artistic expression as healing for military veterans. I went to a "wellness chiropractor" to adjust my attitude and increase the flow of ideas to my brain. The acupuncture flushed out the night sweats and minimized the nightmares.

I ran and walked with my dogs in the sunshine, rain, and snow. I went to the park and festivals, even though sometimes I didn't think I would be able to breathe in the crowd. I farmed and celebrated potluck dinners.

I educated college students about my experiences. We, the veterans and civilian allies, wrote and created art and combat paper. Above all, I had a community—*we* created community. However, there are times that the reminder of failure still plagues me.

There is still more to be done.

The wars go on and the veterans continue to be misunderstood, lost, addicted, homeless, suicidal, homicidal, and traumatized by their communities and the system set up to help them, the VA.

The Boston bombings validated my greatest fear of bombs blowing up on the streets in the USA. For a while, it was like, *finally*, after searching all these years for bombs in the road, scanning and scanning, reliving convoy after convoy—after all these years, it happened ... just like it used to every day in Iraq.

Now *my* war had truly come home. I thought my core broke.

But in my moment of despair, my core simply shifted to:

A light shining on my map for hope.

The war *is* with me, a *part* of me, but it is does not have to consume me. It does not have to be a burden or weight to be carried.

The war can be a thought that drives me to create.

Or the war can disappear completely in those moments reading poetry on the stage or in the dog park.

My lesson about war,

OUR LESSON TOGETHER.

Change your perception of trauma.

Challenge your mind to think differently about war, by channeling the emotion into something that works to help you feel better—empowered—and not to follow the path toward self-destruction.

The lessons I learned after war are:

Healing is not a job.

Speaking the truth is an honor, especially if I can represent for those who cannot speak.

Writing is my gift.

Most of all, I had to change the perception of my purpose ...

I had to forgive myself for sacrificing my humanity to war,

To live and come home.

Eye of the Tiger
Jessica Gimeno

I WAS A JUNIOR IN COLLEGE. It was the second consecutive day that I had spent in bed. I was on a steady diet of cereal and potato chips. A box of Kleenex and unopened textbooks were lying on my bed. If you added a pint of Ben and Jerry's, it would have been the post-breakup scene in any romantic comedy. But, in my case, nothing had "happened." I did not go through a breakup or an argument with a friend or fail an exam. This was yet another sporadic episode of depression.

Bipolar disorder does not care about your deadlines. I had homework to finish and I was competing with my Speech Team at Nationals in a few days. We would be traveling to Long Beach, California. Realizing I would not get any work done, I turned on the television. AMC was running a *Rocky* marathon. I stumbled upon *Rocky III*. Apollo Creed was telling Rocky he needed to get the "eye of the tiger back." Clubber Lang had KO'd Rocky in their first fight, and now they were training for the rematch.

I'd always assumed Rocky was a "guys' movie." But suddenly, it hit me like a bolt of lightning. I was Rocky, and Rocky's opponents were my depression. Even though I was down, I was not out.

That week, I did not win anything at Nationals, but I competed. And I finished my homework.

That bipolar episode happened two years after my diagnosis. My friend Dina's suicide precipitated my diagnosis. Dina had bipolar disorder. When she died, I realized I might also have this disease, and maybe that was why she had understood my mood swings better than anyone else.

I went to the library and read up on the symptoms—and recognized half of them. Since my teen years, I've fought inexplicable bouts of depression marked by crying spells, difficulty concentrating, and suicidal thoughts. Those episodes could last anywhere from hours to weeks.

Just as bizarrely as the episodes came, they disappeared and were replaced with happiness or periods of insomnia, racing thoughts, and great artistic inspiration.

A week after Danielle's death, I saw the campus psychiatrist, who immediately diagnosed me with bipolar disorder. I also sought a second opinion, which confirmed the diagnosis. The diagnosis was the beginning of freedom after years of fighting a faceless, nameless enemy. But it was not a panacea for my problems.

Learning how to manage bipolar disorder was a process. In fact, I missed a final exam when I was a transfer student at Northwestern University during my sophomore year. But slowly, I added more tools to my bipolar survival kit, including medication, talk therapy, building a support network of family and friends, sleeping on time, and maintaining a routine. One of those tools was Rocky. When I would wake up depressed or get anxious before a test, I would watch Rocky's fights.

I graduated *cum laude* from Northwestern with two majors. At the end of my college career, I was a National Quarter-Finalist in Extemporaneous Speaking and a State Champion and National Semi-Finalist in Impromptu Speaking.

Bipolar disorder was not my only foe. I was diagnosed with polycystic ovarian syndrome (PCOS) at nineteen. When I was twenty-four, Myasthenia Gravis, (MG) a neuromuscular autoimmune hurricane disease, invaded my life. MG attacked most parts of my body. Within four months, I went from practicing yoga five days a week to not being able to feel my legs. I underwent several medical procedures and was bedridden for over a year. I heard about MG patients in wheelchairs, and I feared being paralyzed. Thankfully, that didn't happen. Today, I carry a cane.

For the past seven years, I have awakened feeling tired and in pain every day. When I wake up, I play Survivor's "Eye of the Tiger," strap on my Rocky boxing gloves, and pray for strength. I tell myself, "I can do everything through Him who gives me strength."

People often ask me what it is like to live with five illnesses. I see myself as Rocky and my five diseases as Rocky's different opponents. Bipolar disorder is my Apollo Creed. PCOS is Ivan Drago. MG is Mason Dixon. Asthma is Clubber Lang. And, finally, psoriasis is Tommy Gunn.

God bless Sylvester Stallone for creating a film franchise that spanned four decades. Boxing has become a metaphor for my struggles. Much like chronic illness, boxing is brutal and barbaric. Fighting an illness (or five) is not a team sport. I can have people in my corner, but my body is the only one that absorbs the pain.

I am a writer and health activist, but my day job is coaching high school debate. A few months ago, we were at the state championship, which was held at a community college with a large campus. At one point, the other coaches and I reached an impasse. To get from one building to another, I had to climb a long flight of stairs. I closed my eyes and imagined the stairs were the steps of the Philadelphia Museum of Art that Stallone made famous. There was no Rocky victory dance when I got to the top, but I made it.

I realized that I had been using visualization as a coping tool for years. Until that moment, I'd never had a word for it. First, visualizing helped me fight depression, and now, my physical disability. You can call it "the eye of the tiger" or whatever you want, but visualization enables me to write my own story, every day.

As long as I can see victory, I can fight one more round.

i

....

Stigma & My Life's Epiphany: A Short Play in Six Acts

Rick Strait

WHEN MOST PEOPLE hear the word "epiphany" they think the definition involves a "sudden awareness." But my life's epiphany actually came in six different steps.

As far back as I can remember, I had a sadness that I couldn't explain, often wishing I was never born or not alive. I had a good childhood with great parents, so it was difficult for me to understand why I was so sad. I kept it to myself for most of my life.

In 1993, my younger brother, who was seventeen at the time, was killed in a car accident. This traumatic event took me to a whole new level of sadness and I went from wishing I wasn't alive to contemplating suicide. When the thoughts of wanting to die got stronger than my desire to live, I sought help.

First, I talked to a pastor who could only muster the sentiment that he would pray for me. Next, I talked to a military chaplain. "Pull yourself together," he grunted. "There are people who have it a lot worse than you." I left that office feeling lower than I ever had in my life—and that weekend, I attempted suicide.

In the aftermath, I thanked God daily (and still do) that the attempt didn't work, but I was still very sad. Although I still struggled with suicidal thoughts, I knew I wouldn't attempt suicide again. However, I didn't know how to make the suicidal and depressive thoughts go away.

Epiphany: Act I

While in college, I took some psychology classes and began to learn about depression. I soon found out *"I'm not the only one who feels this way."* Learning about others didn't take away my pain—I still didn't know what to do about it—but I thought I could learn to help others. I continued with college and eventually obtained my master's degree in Clinical Counseling. Soon, I began working with others who were depressed and felt hopeless.

Epiphany: Act II

I quickly realized that *"Helping others helped me feel better."* However, I felt like a fraud. I encouraged others to openly discuss their mental illness with their loved ones and not be ashamed. Yet at the same time, I kept my own mental illness to myself and struggled in silence.

While working for a behavior health unit with acute mental health clients, I had a supervisor, Erin, who had lost her brother to suicide. I still struggled with depression, and I'd recently found out a friend had attempted suicide. I knew I had to do more to help myself and others.

Erin and I discussed the need to create better education and more awareness in our community, so we decided to organize a Suicide Prevention and Awareness Conference.

Epiphany: Act III

Putting on this conference helped me realize that *"Educating others about suicide helps me feel like I can make a difference."* It felt good to help others—but I continued to live with stigma by keeping my battle with depression to myself.

By 2014, I had helped organize three suicide prevention and awareness conferences for the hospital where I worked. I'd spoken at two conferences about suicide prevention and I'd become a Mental Health First Aid instructor. I felt I was really starting to make a difference, in spite of my silence about my own depression.

In the fall of 2014, I was asked to speak about mental health and suicide prevention at the Cape Girardeau Out of the Darkness Walk. I agreed, but I struggled with what to present. Finally, I decided to share my personal story—but first, I needed to tell a few co-workers about my depression and suicide attempt, in private.

Epiphany: Act IV

"My friends and co-workers didn't judge me; they supported me," and some even shared with me their own personal struggles. I spoke with my adult children and my parents, and I explained what I was planning on sharing at the walk. Each member of my family was supportive.

The day came when I stood in front of more than three hundred people—friends, coworkers, and a lot of strangers—and shared my story.

Epiphany: Act V

Just after finishing my speech, I realized for the first time that "*I couldn't truly be free until I accepted and talked about my own illness.*" I could never take back the words I'd said to that crowd of on-lookers—and I was okay with it. And since then, I have continued to share my story and have found nothing but tremendous support.

Epiphany: Act VI

Recently, someone asked me if I was upset with the people who I had turned to for help, people like the pastor or the military chaplain, who didn't help me. It took me but a split second to reply. "*People can't help if they aren't educated and comfortable talking about mental illness and suicide.*"

And that's why I share my story: so that if you or someone you know needs help with their mental illness or is experiencing suicidal thinking—reaching out for and receiving help won't take an epiphany in six parts. It'll happen in a matter of seconds.

Lived Experience
With Suicide

"BE KIND, for everyone you meet is fighting a hard battle."
- Philo

i

....

The Madness Monster
Judy Thrasher

T HE "MONSTER" ENTERED OUR LIVES so furtively that it went undetected by anyone until it had completely enveloped Allen's mind.

Allen and I had spent ten years of "normal" marriage together. We lived in a "normal" country home and had a "normal" garden. We had three "normal" children. Everything was "normal"… that is, until the "monster" moved in.

That "monster" was schizophrenia, a chemical imbalance of the brain. That "monster" took control of Allen's mind, despite his attempts to fight it off.

The first time I recall something being awry was during a trip to Florida with our three small children in March 1994. Although Allen had always been a moody person, his behavior during this vacation went beyond "normal" boundaries. Allen displayed paranoia toward everyone we met. He verbalized fears that these strangers were out to somehow hurt our children. Allen, normally a friendly and outgoing man, refused to carry a conversation with anyone. He became so fear-ful of the surroundings that we left a day earlier than planned.

During the six months that followed, Allen displayed periods of both anxiety and normalcy. The summer months were filled with fam-ily activities and "normal" days in our "normal" country home. But as the summer came to an end, so did our last "normal" months with Al-len, who had gone into a mode of high anxiety, over-activity, and very little sleep.

Soon, autumn came, and it seemed to trigger the worst of Allen's episodes—like when he explained to me in detail about an incident at the factory where he worked. There was a labor dispute over a job he currently held and it escalated out of control. Allen would pace, talk to himself, and lie awake all night in deep thought. He told me that these behaviors were due to the stress at work.

Allen called me from work one afternoon, but his words were mak-ing no sense. I immediately called his supervisor and asked if there was any way this work issue could be resolved. I explained that I was concerned about Allen's mental state. His foreman replied, "Look, I don't know what kind of work problems you're talking about. He needs to fix the problems he's having at home!" I was stunned when I suddenly realized there had been no problem at work. There had been no problems at home. The only problems were those planted in his mind by the "monster."

When Allen arrived home, a crisis intervention team was consult-ed. Allen was assessed by specialists and found to be dangerous to himself and to others. He was hospitalized in psychiatric intensive care an hour away from home.

An avid hunter, Allen owned several guns, which I removed from our home while he was hospitalized. During times of instability, he frequently asked for his guns. Though his intentions were unknown, I lived in fear for my life twenty-four hours a day, seven days a week.

As I was busy raising our three small children, I had the additional burden of trying to "get my husband back" from the horrible monster that had taken Allen from us. So many times I recall looking deeply into his empty eyes and begging him to return to us. I had been left to care for this "stranger" who'd been sent to take his place.

Our lives during those four years of instability with Allen were filled with both PTA meetings and doctor's appointments; mountains of medication and our children's slumber parties; hospitalizations and gymnastics—a never-ending balance between the "normal" and the "abnormal."

There was the public image that the community saw on our better days, and the dark, chaotic side that filled all of the other times. Our world revolved around Allen's illness. The only consistency in our lives was inconsistency. The "monster" was in control of Allen's body and soul, and thus in control of our entire family.

The "monster" had now convinced Allen that people were watching him and wanted to hurt him. It made him physically react to these threats that did not even exist. These behaviors were wearing our family down, and had certainly taken their toll on me. I was forced to try to return some sort of normalcy back to our family without my husband.

We separated, and Allen returned to stay with his parents. My three small children and I would try to be a "normal" family again—an arrangement that seemed to be the lesser of two evils.

For four months, Allen stayed with his parents as we desperately tried to make the best of this tragic situation. As the summer of 1998 came to an end, Allen's delusions and paranoia were heightening. None of the medications could control the hold that the "monster" had on him. Life became too difficult and the thoughts too dark.

Allen made a decision to bring to an end the "monster" who lived only in his mind. He longed for a serenity that was no longer an option on this Earth.

During his inner turmoil, Allen found the only handgun he owned, loaded it, and sent his parents out to run an errand. They were gone only thirty minutes, but it only took a moment. There were no explanations. There were no farewells. All that was left were those who loved him and many unanswered questions. We're without Allen ... but Allen is without his "monster."

Since that beautiful autumn day fifteen years ago, the colorful leaves of fall do not seem as bright. However, life's darkest days have shown me just how precious life is and how it can change in a heartbeat. It has taught me to live every single moment as if it were my last. It has made me laugh harder, cry harder, and love harder. It has made me more understanding of others, since we are all fighting our own demons.

I will continue on as an advocate for those who have lost their ability to advocate for themselves, and help others in their battles against "monsters."

Music: A Bridge to and Through My Soul

Jennifer Burton

AS A TEENAGER OF THE 1980S, my inner wild child has always been a part of who I am. I proudly proclaim myself a music-obsessed soul. It was my senior year in high school when I attended my first rock concert. Motley Crüe was in their heyday when my friends and I traveled to St. Louis to witness them rock the house at the legendary Kiel Auditorium. That concert was the loudest performance I have ever experienced; my ears rang for days with guitar riffs.

Growing up with two sisters, six and eight years older than me, my love of music began at a young age. My eldest sister bought me the soundtrack to "A Star is Born" with Barbara Streisand and Kris Kristofferson for my twelfth birthday.

Music speaks to me on a spiritual level. Throughout my life it has been a medium of communication, a way to express feelings, to heal struggling relationships, and to dance like no one is watching (and even when they are). During the darkest period of my life, my relationship with music would literally save me.

Twelve years ago, my husband Mark and I had just become proud parents of a fourth child—another beautiful daughter. I have always referred to our home as "Hectic House" and we were overjoyed with our new family of six.

I distinctly remember the phone ringing one morning after we had just sent our other three children off to school. As he answered the phone, I realized that something I had always known could happen … had happened. As tears rolled down my husband's face, before I could even scream the words "What's wrong, is it Ronnie?" I knew the answer … Ronnie had taken his own life.

Ronnie and I met and fell in love in high school when I was fifteen and he seventeen. Three weeks into our new and exciting love affair, Ronnie dropped thirty pounds and soon after was diagnosed with a very severe case of Type I diabetes. At fifteen, I became a partner in fighting this terrible disease with my new boyfriend.

We eventually married and had two sons. Our relationship was tumultuous at times, and over the years, through the struggles he faced with fighting his disease—and later, an undiagnosed and untreated depressive disorder—things became unbearable. I had to make a choice between being a good mother and staying in a tempestuous relationship that could damage my sons' future stability.

Ronnie had threatened suicide during our relationship many times. I wasn't sure if he would be okay if I left, but I knew I had to do what was best for our sons. That is why when the phone rang on that fateful morning, I knew in my soul what had happened before my husband, Mark, could tell me.

My young sons were in fourth and sixth grades at the time. They loved their daddy and had spent many fun weekends with him. Many years had passed since our divorce, and my husband Mark and I enjoyed more of a familial relationship with Ronnie than the unfriendly dynamic one would expect between exes. We all loved him.

Bringing our sons home from school to tell them the news was gut-wrenching. I was given the best advice of my life before they arrived. Both my pastor and the children's pediatrician urged me "tell them the truth of how their daddy died."

They came running in the door knowing something was terribly wrong because Mark had picked them up early from school. With tears already streaming down their faces, I gave them the news. "Daddy has died."

"How?" they screamed. "Why?"

"Daddy's mind was not working correctly. Just like you can catch a cold and become very sick, sometimes the brain can become sick and not work correctly. He shot himself."

From that moment on, my number one priority was the emotional well-being of our sons. Our hearts were broken at the loss of Ronnie and for the horror that our innocent, beautiful sons had to face.

It was easy to busy myself with my family of six. It was easy to stuff my own grief and survivor guilt deep within my soul and forge ahead as self-appointed savior of my children. Making sure they were "okay" in spite of this trauma became my mission.

Sure, there were many times when, after tucking the kids in bed, I would retreat to my computer, put on my headphones, pour one, two … four glasses of wine, and just lose myself in music. But the sun would come up the next day and, hangover or not, I would forge ahead.

Music was the very beginning of a means to process what my soul was begging me to deal with. But I didn't realize that by pairing music with excessive alcohol, I was ignoring my own grief. My avoidance of dealing with my emotional pain would bring me to a very dark place years later.

A once optimistic, self-reliant gal slowly became a self-destructive person I didn't know. As my children began to grow up and my sons eventually went away to college, my self-destructive drinking became worse. I would stay up late at night, drinking heavily, listening to music and singing (badly, I might add) at the top of my lungs with my headphones on. I was purging some sort of demon that I didn't understand. At times, I was surprised the next morning to find that I was still alive.

I begged God to help me. I didn't understand why I was doing what I was doing. I had dear friends who were put in place in my life during my early descent into self-destruction. A struggle such as mine couldn't be hidden for long. At the point of begging for answers, desperately wanting a solution to and escape from the self-destructive pattern, I asked a friend, who also happened to be a counselor, "Why am I doing this?"

She answered, "Jennifer, you are in pain!"

Another precious friend helped to keep my self-loathing above an unbearable place. I remember him saying to me, "You have everything inside yourself to beat this." These friends, along with many others, came alongside with support and love, and no judgment in their eyes or hearts.

My survivor's guilt had turned into self-loathing and binge drinking. My soul was crying out for help, begging and finally demanding for me to deal with my own pain. Music was the medium my soul used to wake me.

Today, I am no longer in that place of self-destruction, through the help of therapy, dear friends, and family, as well as my ability to be honest with others and myself about the truth of my struggle. Music allowed my soul to process what my brain wasn't able to accept, and I am a person I once again know and love. Our Hectic House family is thriving and stronger than ever, and I am so thankful for surviving the painful journey.

In literal terms, a "musical bridge" can be described as a contrasting section in music, which prepares for a return to the section of the original material. My musical bridge carried me through my darkest journey with the language of love, hope, and faith, right back to the "original material" of me.

Pain With a Purpose

Barb Smith

IT WAS A BEAUTIFUL DAY as I drove home from the beaches of Tawas, Michigan. I noticed my then-boyfriend in my rear view mirror, motioning for me to pull over. I did, and he walked up to the car looking devastated. He had been trying get in touch with me all day.

"You need to get home," he said. I asked why, but he wouldn't tell me. I knew it wasn't good, but being strong-willed as I am, I wouldn't let it go until he said those horrible words. "John took his life."

John was twenty-years-old, my older brother by two years. He was my friend, confident, and the prankster in the family—and I decided this was just another one of those pranks.

I drove as fast as I could to get to my parents' house. All I could hear when I walked in was my mother's wail—a mournful howl that pierced all the way through to my heart. Mom was sitting at the kitchen table where we had many family dinners—we were a good family, and this wasn't supposed to happen in good, Christian families.

My seven other siblings were all standing in silence—no one spoke. But I wanted answers. I wanted to know where he was and I demanded to see him. He would not do this. He would never hurt himself or anyone in our family. This was not true, it couldn't be, dear God, let me wake from this nightmare. It was like watching a movie in slow motion.

I found out John had gone to both his friend's and his girlfriend's house, saying he couldn't live without her. Both of them tried to find him, but waited to call my family. By then he had driven to his favorite hunting spot to end his life. He stopped on the way to write us a "note" saying how much he loved us, but that he hated the world and he wanted to end his pain.

Recently, John had been laid off from his job, and his friend had canceled their big parachuting trip—but the final disappointment for him was his girlfriend breaking up with him. In my eighteen-year-old mind, I thought, "You get another girlfriend, you get another job, you reschedule with your buddy, but *you don't kill yourself.*"

So my grief journey began, one for which I was not prepared. I searched for answers to the "whys" by going to conferences, researching suicide, and educating myself as much as I could. During the 1980s there was very little written about suicide, and not many people were talking about it.

The day John ended his pain, our pain began. I was determined to not let this destroy me as it did my father. Tragedies can make you bitter or better—it's a choice. I was going to be a better friend, mentor, and person in every way. When someone suicides, it changes you, but it doesn't have to destroy you.

I started a support group, "Survivors of Suicide," for loved ones left behind. I learned so much from the participants who were willing to share their stories—but still this wasn't enough. I thought, "We can sit around this table talking about the 'whys' and our grief for the next twenty-five years, or we can take our grief and educate others."

I got certified in the Yellow Ribbon Suicide Prevention Program and have since spoken to more than 65,000 people about the warning signs and risk factors of suicide. I empower teens and ask participants to come forward after the presentation to ask for help for themselves or someone they have a concern about. We de-stigmatize mental illness, one of the major factors in a suicide.

I trained for our Victims Services unit, where I have the opportunity to be with the newly bereaved in the early hours of a tragedy, so families like mine are better equipped than I was for questions like "Where do I turn next?" and "How do I prepare for something like this?"

Being recognized as an "expert" in suicide prevention and intervention, I thought I could help prevent every suicide within my region of the world. But one evening while sitting at the dinner table with my family, my phone rang. It was my brother Larry yelling into the phone, "We need you. Jackie killed herself."

Not again. This time I was angry. How dare she? My own sister-in-law. She didn't have the right. She knew about the work I do. I took this personally. I had "missed" the signs I was so well-trained to recognize. The first time I was ignorant to suicide, but this time I should have known.

I had to quit my work in suicide prevention. How could I teach others when I couldn't even save my own family?

But not long after Jackie's death, I received a call from my friend Julie, whose fourteen-year-old daughter was talking about ending her own life. And so, I went into intervention mode, and I became passionate about suicide prevention once again. I was determined to help save her. I strongly advocated that she get professional help, and a month later, she called to thank me for saving her life.

Helping to save Julie's daughter taught me a lesson about myself and Jackie: even though we are aware of the signs of suicide and do everything right, we will still lose people.

And though my brother John left this earth, he will never truly leave us. He will continue to touch the lives of thousands of people. The greatest way to honor someone's life is to do good work in his or her memory. Share who they were and the gifts they left you. Whether it's being a coach, mentor, or musician, do it with love and passion from the bottom of your heart, for it's through you that they will live on and touch the lives of others.

An Unexpected Lesson From a "Great" Dane

Ashley Kowalczyk

EVERYONE HAS A DIFFERENT WAY to describe depression. To me, depression is a dirty grey, worn, hole-ridden blanket that I've had wrapped around my body tightly, even though it doesn't keep me warm at all. I started struggling with depression when I was twelve years old and have dealt with it in varying degrees ever since. The most wrapped up in depression that I have been was when I was nineteen years old.

The story actually begins when I was fourteen, attending Rockford Christian Camp, where I met Dane. He was different from all of the other boys, with his black band t-shirts and piercings. As a blossoming "Emo" girl, I was attracted to him instantly. But even more, he had a contagious laugh and the biggest heart of anyone I had ever met. Dane had this magical ability to show a person a mirror featuring all of the good and beauty that they had inside of themselves. I fell for him fast.

When I was fifteen, we started dating. He made me feel beautiful and special, which was a strange feeling for a teenage girl with depression and a crippling self-image.

However, Dane had his own insecurities and struggled with a deeper depression than my own. He had self-injured and attempted suicide several times during his short life. We were together for almost a year before I broke up with him. I didn't know how to deal with my own issues, let alone someone else's.

While we were apart, Dane experimented with drugs and eventually became addicted to heroin. After an attempted overdose, he decided to turn his life around. We reconnected, and at my insistence, Dane was honest with me about all that he was struggling with. Eventually, we started dating again.

Our relationship had its ups and downs as Dane fought with his demons, the occasional relapse, and the belief that he wasn't good enough for me, let alone anyone else. But we loved each other, and he asked me marry him once I had graduated from college. Even through all of his pain and suffering, Dane never stopped seeing the good in people or being the best friend everyone needed, and he made me feel incredibly happy and loved.

When I graduated from high school and started attending Bradley University to pursue a degree in teaching, the only people prouder than him were my parents. Dane had also started working to become a counselor to help people struggling with the same issues that he had.

On March 11, 2010, shortly before his twentieth birthday and after six months of being completely clean, Dane lost his struggle with heroin. I soon felt my depression blanket encase me so tightly that I felt that I couldn't breathe. My best friend was gone. Sleep was foreign to me, but I couldn't make myself get out of bed.

While I managed to finish my freshman year of college, I was completely lost. Why couldn't he have kept a shred of the love he held for other people, for himself? My anger toward God and Dane was only matched by my hopelessness, and I started coping in unhealthy ways.

A few months after Dane's death, I saw a Facebook post from To Write Love on Her Arms (TWOLHA), an organization whose mission statement is: "… dedicated to presenting hope and finding help for people struggling with depression, addiction, self-injury, and suicide. TWLOHA exists to encourage, inform, inspire, and also to invest directly into treatment and recovery."

A light bulb switched on in my head. Even though Dane was gone, I could try to help people who struggled as he had, and connect with people who had felt pain the way I had. I contacted TWLOHA to start a chapter at Bradley University, and they connected me with a young woman who was also interested in starting a chapter at the school. We worked hard that year and formed a strong core group of people who were accepting and wanting to connect with other struggling people.

For three years, I was the president of our chapter. We held meetings discussing issues related to mental illness. We organized concerts and invited speakers. During this time, I started counseling and began sharing my own struggles with people that I trusted. The depression blanket I had carried, once wrapped so tightly around me, began to loosen as I worked through putting an end to my unhealthy coping habits. I made amends with God and found strength in the people who loved me so dearly that they would not let me give up.

Even though Dane has been gone four years, I still miss him and feel the impact of his love. His life and death have taught me that I am stronger than I ever knew, and I can rely on the people I love to help hold me up when I can't stand—help we all need from time to time. I also learned to truly love and see people for all the beauty and good that they are.

I needed to learn to see the beauty and good inside of myself, something I was not used to doing. I am trying to live my life without judging others, to see people the way that Dane saw them, and to look at myself the way that he saw me.

As I finish my semester of student teaching, I am terrified at the thought of graduating, but I'm excited to start the next chapter. My blanket of depression is looser than it has been in years. I know that I am strong enough to make it through anything and will be a teacher who incorporates a true sense of community and self-love into my classroom.

i

....

You Can Come Back
Jennifer Haussler Garing

WAS THIRTEEN THE FIRST TIME I tried to kill myself. Luckily, or unluckily, I lacked a certain sophistication with pharmaceuticals. I awoke the next morning with a horrid hangover and the awful realization that no one had noticed my attempt. It seemed ridiculous to point it out. After all, it wouldn't further my cause. I hadn't done it to gain attention. I was looking for an exit. So I quietly moved on, working most of my teen years in a chain drugstore and stifling my urge to purchase sleeping pills.

It was in college that I was finally diagnosed and treated for the depression that had rattled me for so many years. They carefully doled out my medication so that I wasn't able to overdose, but they just didn't understand. Why would you use the means to your salvation to affect your demise? There is an etiquette to suicide. At least, for me there was. But they never believed me.

Perhaps it was because they knew what depression can do to a person. Depression is a life-wrecker. It swings in and topples your life and leaves you buried in collateral damage—in no condition to clean up the mess. As you lie there, you see nothing but darkness with no memories of past happiness, love, hope, or sunlight. Why would you think it would ever be any different?

Suicide becomes the seemingly rational option—the glowing red exit sign. You have to listen very hard for that oh-so-quiet voice of reason buried somewhere in the rubble, the one that says, "You can come back."

You'd think that it would get easier once you come to understand it. But it doesn't. Being suicidal almost becomes a steady state, and looking for lethal objects becomes like looking for an emergency exit—your just-in-case solution. It's a terrifying way to live. I used to be able to devise a suicide plan with any three objects. Name them. It might not be quick and it might not be pretty, but I could do it. That's how far gone I was.

Regardless of what my mind had planned for me, I fought to stay in control. But my mind always had some evil trick, some plan to send me off the rails. With each episode, it would have some new play that it would turn loose on me.

During an episode in my mid-thirties, I had one thought that nagged at me continuously. I was in probably my fifth or sixth life-shattering episode of depression. My mind bombarded me with questions. How many times are you going to have to claw your way out of this same hole? How much time are you going to have to spend picking up the pieces? How much do you have to lose? When do you get to say you've given it your best shot, but you're tired and you're done?

I finally voiced these thoughts to my therapist and he had one simple answer: "Not yet."

In my late thirties, my depression became treatment-resistant, and I sank into another episode. Although I had learned that you cannot control your mind, I had found that you can control your surroundings, your support system, and your work situation. What could have been a life destroyer, wasn't. I took leave from work. My mother and father came to help me, and my close friends and coworkers were somewhat prepared for the fallout.

I remember, during this particular depression, asking my mother if I had ever been happy, because I had no recollection of it. We sat there at my kitchen table, both wracking our brains for a solid memory of my happiness. Truth be told, my mother has the worst memory for these types of things, and I should have asked anyone else. But what we came up with was a piece of pure magic.

It was a Sunday afternoon when I had visited the Lewis Ginter Botanical Garden. They had a butterfly exhibit in part of the conservatory. Late in the afternoon, I was alone in the exhibit. I remember sitting on a bench, staring at the beautiful creatures fluttering around me and regaining, for the first time in years, that childhood sense of wonder—that feeling that anything is possible. And remembering those emotions, I could see beyond the darkness and hear that quietest of voices: "You can come back."

It helped that, even in the depths of depression, I had myself anchored to the outside world, which included my parents, my sister, my nephews, my friends, my cat, and my dog. By this point, I was bound and determined that this depression that had taken so much from me would not get the balance of my life, and I would not become an accomplice in my own demise.

I no longer fear suicide. There are things I feel unsafe around—high, open balconies, exposed beams, straight-edged razors—but I don't think it makes me less of a person to avoid such things. I know my limits and I just don't like how these things make me feel. It's kind of like how I feel on roller coasters.

These days, I anchor myself to my surroundings. I hold tightly to the things I love. I keep reminders of those things that give me hope and remind me that the world is full of wonder and possibility—because I know there will be days when I need to be reminded of these facts. I will do everything in my power to prevent these days from happening, but I know they will come.

The one thing I will always be sure of is that the only constant in life is change. No matter how bad things get, they will always get better, even if they have to get worse first. I cling to that.

i

....

Making it Work
Dana Sayre

WHEN I THINK OF SUICIDE, I don't think of my attempt. I think of life in the aftermath. Specifically, I think of the day after I got out of the hospital. My sister came to stay with me for a week to help me get my life together for the fall semester of my junior year of college.

I think of us walking up the hill to my campus apartment. Of her making black bean and corn salad for me to take to the Fine Arts Department picnic. Of us sitting on the couch, and her telling me that the opposite of suicide is revolution.

Even now, I struggle the most when I think I'm not making enough of a difference or a contribution to society. Or when there seem to be too many problems in the world, or even just my life, to begin to know how to fix any of them.

It makes some logical sense. If the status is not quo (to quote Dr. Horrible), I can either opt out or try to make it quo.

Not that dichotomies are ever true, either.

{ 153 }

I was reading *Girl, Interrupted* around the time of my suicide attempt. It was comforting to read the words of someone else who'd been there. In the section where she talks about her suicide attempt, the narrator said part of her did die that day—the part of her that wanted to die.

I often feel that way.

It's as if there were two people living inside of me, one of whom wanted to live, and another who did not. It was hard sometimes to tell who was winning.

I believe the reason I think about *after* my suicide attempt, and not before it, is that I'm not the girl who wanted to die.

She's dead. She doesn't exist anymore.

My life started the day I got out of the hospital.

I am someone else—someone who got a second chance and isn't always sure what to do with it. It's hard to make a five-year plan when you thought you'd be dead eight years ago.

I don't always know what this new, alive me wants or needs, but I do my best. It's an odd feeling.

I like big chunks of my life now, but sometimes it doesn't feel like it's really mine, in a way I don't know how to explain. It's like I'm living in an alternate timeline.

It's like the last eight years weren't supposed to happen, and somewhere else, I'm dead in that university apartment bedroom at twenty years old. Except I don't know whose life that was. I only know it's not mine.

Not anymore.

I don't want to sound as if I'm condoning attempted suicide as a means to get past suicidal ideation. I just know there can be this pressure to be okay, or to act okay. And it can all be too much for those of us who really, really aren't okay.

I think what I really wanted then was a break. An escape. To rest. But there are other ways to get that.

Even now, my family doesn't talk about mental health, and they don't believe in therapy. I'm not sure how twenty-year-old me would have gotten to the point of checking myself into the hospital when liver failure wasn't imminent.

But I'm sure someone else could.

In some ways, that week in the hospital was the best week of my life. Because in there, it was finally okay that I wasn't okay.

Being able to be broken can be really liberating.

A break from reality can offer perspective.

I can't explain the shift, even in myself. How does one go from wanting to die to being okay with being alive again?

Having something to live for helped, at first.

I made a promise to my sister that I wouldn't try again. Because I do love her, probably more than anyone else in the world. When she said she didn't know what she'd do without me, I knew the same was true for me.

My closest friends since that time have also struggled with mental illness: anxiety, depression, bipolar ... without meaning to, we seek each other out.

I don't know how to relate to anyone who hasn't stared into the abyss and come out the other side.

I want to be able to offer some advice for how to get from there to here, but I didn't use a map. I was stumbling around in the dark and suddenly found a path underneath my feet again.

I can't explain how I got here. I just know I haven't been back there since.

I do a self-check every once in a while, when I'm feeling really depressed. I think to myself, "Would I rather be dead?" But somehow, no. I always want to keep trying.

I think you just find one thing, literally one thing that might be worth living for, and you live for that thing for an hour, a day, a week. I threw myself into school. Before I knew it, I was living again.

And it was okay.

Life is complicated. It's beautiful and confusing and heartbreaking and confounding and joyful and ridiculous and painful and surprising.

And it's hard. It really is.

Sometimes it feels like things won't get better—on a personal scale or a national or global one.

I think of Samuel Beckett's *Waiting for Godot.* Even when the world is utter shit, if you find a DeeDee or a GoGo, at least you're not wading through it alone.

Love isn't always enough.

But sometimes it is.

I try to find my tribe. I do the best I can. Most of the time, there are enough good things that the bad ones don't make me think of cashing in my chips.

That might not be anyone else's answer.

More Than a Survivor
Marcia Gelman Resnick

I T IS OFTEN SAID, AND I BELIEVE, that you are only as happy as your least happy child. I am a mother who buried three children. My only surviving child had Hodgkin's disease within two years of the death of his brother. Now I am the happiest I have ever been.

Married when I was not quite twenty-one, after a few years, I wanted to have a child. My two older sisters already had children. Every year on Mother's Day, my dad would take the whole family to a hotel to celebrate the mothers in our family. I was the only one who was not a mother, and it hurt.

My first child, a son, was born in February 1974. He lived until the age of twenty-eight. However, he was born severely brain damaged, microcephalic—a condition when a person's brain does not grow. He could not speak, hear, or talk, and was totally unaware of anything. All he had was a strong heart. We kept him at home for about six months and then put him in a home where he could get proper care. I still wasn't really a mother.

{ 157 }

In August 1976, after taking fertility drugs, I gave birth to twins, a boy and a girl. The twins were a little premature, but were doing well in the hospital. They were almost ready to go home when my daughter stopped feeding. The doctors could not figure out what was wrong. They tried absolutely everything, but she was failing. She died when she was three weeks old. I was twenty-eight at the time, picking out a coffin and cemetery plot for my daughter. Thankfully, my son, Doug, did come home.

After all we had been through, we finally had our precious child. I was a mother. Two-and-a-half years later, we were blessed with another healthy son. After all the tragedy, I believed that my share of loss was over, and that my two sons would grow up to be happy, healthy adults ... boy, was I in for a rude awakening.

At the age of twenty-two, on the day his girlfriend broke up with him, my son Doug took his life. We did not see this coming. When people are depressed, many put on a mask. I did not even know that he and his girlfriend were having any problems. Whenever I asked him how he was, his answer was "excellent."

How does a parent feel when they lose a child to suicide? I felt like my world had come to an end. I was just a normal, regular person. I had buried one child, and one child was severely brain damaged. Why me? I was on a planet all by myself. How could this happen to me? What would I do now? I was totally clueless as to what to do to continue on with my life without Doug.

My friends helped me find support groups with other "normal" parents like me who had also lost their children to suicide. They were on this strange new planet with me. I went to every in-person support group available. I joined an online support group, Parents of Suicides (POS). We grieved together, we supported each other, and we understood each other. We were in a club that no one wanted to be in.

I gave up my law practice. I had to take care of both myself and my only surviving child.

Then my surviving son was diagnosed with Hodgkin's disease. We had to get through this as well, and we did. He went through chemotherapy, which was successful. He was only twenty-two, but he handled the situation with grace and humor.

I have buried three children. It is still surreal when I go to the cemetery and see the names of my three children on graves. No parent should ever have to see that.

Where am I now? I still am active in POS, and many of my closest friends are people I met through that group. I have traveled to New Zealand, Australia, and South Africa several times, and to Georgia (U.S.A.) often, to spend time with my fellow "sisters" who have lost children to suicide.

I have facilitated a support group for "Parents Who Lost Children to Suicide" for nearly five years. I participate in a volunteer outreach program run by the American Foundation for Suicide Prevention (AFSP). When a newly bereaved family requests services, two outreach volunteers go to their home and offer support and guidance. My husband and I participate every year in an eighteen-mile overnight walk for AFSP— a nonprofit organization that raises money for suicide education, research, and support.

Why do I do this? There were wonderful people who helped me get through the shock of losing Doug and who helped me to start living again. Now I want to be there for others who are just starting out on this journey of grief. Giving back and helping others is the only way to give meaning to Doug's death.

Who am I now? I recently turned sixty-five. To celebrate my birthday, I had a girls' weekend at a spa, and we had a great time. I love to travel, go to the theater, ski, and play tennis. I have a wonderful family and dear friends.

Best of all, my son and his wife gave me the most amazing gift ever—a grandson who is now three months old. I could not be happier. Life is good right now.

Peter

Kenya Casey

....

A S I TYPE, MY EYES swell with tears, and memories I have tucked away for rainy days resurface. We were kindred spirits, my uncle and I—free-spirited, creative, and a bit on the strange side. We were two peas in a pod. We understood one another.

He escaped to Africa through literature and music, and I had the privilege of traveling to those same places that occupied his dreams and bookshelves. He was the historian/philosopher type, a relentless talker. When we discussed Africa, he would give me the history lesson and I would share my experience of everyday culture—the food, the people and the music.

Besides my mother, there was never a family member who understood my quirkiness more than Uncle Peter. No explanations needed. But we hadn't lived in the same city since I was nine years old. Separated by my parent's divorce, I spent more than a decade without seeing my dad's side of the family, Uncle Peter included. It was only through phone calls and letters that we remained close.

Uncle Peter was the stereotypical Bay Area bohemian and the black sheep of the family. In the late 1970s, he moved to California and began practicing holistic healing through herbs, stones, and essential oils. Gradually, voodoo became a familiar acquaintance—a far cry from his Midwestern upbringing.

Many would brush off his eccentric behavior as "Peter being Peter"—but at some point, the quirkiness transformed into paranoia. Over the years, the stories became more elaborate and fanatical. My social work training had prepared me to engage others with mental illness, but Uncle Peter was not within my reach logistically, emotionally, or mentally. The slow train wreck seemed imminent. I knew heartbreak, a crisis, or some kind of tragedy was on the horizon.

At least six months prior to his death, I pleaded with my godfather and father to intervene and get Uncle Peter some help. I was not close to my uncle's wife and did not feel comfortable reaching out. My godfather tried to help by contacting Uncle Peter's therapist, but due to confidentiality policies, nothing could be done.

The last time I saw Uncle Peter was in June of 2009 at my godfather's memorial service. Uncle Peter's transition from this earth was seemingly already in motion. At the memorial service, I placed on the altar a picture taken on my last trip to California—it was my godfather, Uncle Peter, and me, all together. As I laid the photo down, my instincts told me to pick it back up. The gesture felt like a foreshadowing of my uncle's death.

When I received the call two months later that Uncle Peter had died by suicide, I instantly flashed back to the photo. Devastation consumed me, but I was not surprised.

In the Black community, we do not openly discuss mental illness and suicide. Not only do we avoid the topics within our family, but it is often considered off-limits to discuss with outsiders. Growing up, I remember people within my community saying, "Black people do not commit suicide; only white people have that privilege."

A mentor of mine recently explained that, historically, Black people were more concerned about survival and did not have the luxury to process their own suffering. We look at suffering as a part of the Black experience.

The way people in my community have rationalized suicide is by dismissing the possible existence of mental illness. They put more emphasis on the person's inability to handle their circumstances, and more weight on seeking spiritual guidance from the church rather than seeking help from a mental health practitioner.

In an effort to heal and process my uncle's death, I had to find meaning and work to break the stigma associated with suicide and mental illness. A month after his death, I signed up for a six-month grief and loss support group. I joined the American Foundation for Suicide Prevention's Out of the Darkness walk and participated in the National Day for Suicide Loss forum.

Shame and guilt clouded over my uncle's death, which made everything more complex. My father asked me not to discuss the circumstances of the suicide with anyone. Understanding the immense pain my father was experiencing, I wanted to respect his wishes, but I also felt that secrecy would help no one. I pleaded with him to share his story in hopes that it would help him work through his feelings and that it might help someone else who had experienced suicide loss.

A year later, he participated on his own in the Oakland, California Out of the Darkness walk. I had never been so proud of my dad. His guilt seemed less pervasive and acceptance was honing in on him. The walk helped suppress the loneliness, even if it was only momentarily.

I have several friends who suffer from depression and I have had former students with clinically diagnosed mental illnesses. I keep suicide prevention resources within reach and continue to advocate for people to seek behavioral health counseling.

After losing my Uncle Peter, I made numerous friends who have lost loved ones to suicide. Their loving spirit and passion for healing is a constant reminder that healing is a journey, not a destination. Throughout this journey we must keep sharing and keep walking, without judgment. We must know when to reach out for support and care.

My charge is to break the silence and speak openly about death by suicide. I will not let my uncle's death be in vain.

i'

....

LGBT

"TO ME BEAUTY is about being comfortable in your own skin. It's about knowing and accepting who you are."

  - Ellen Degeneres

Risking Your Heart to Find Your Home

Jamie Myre

SOMETIMES IT'S HARD TO KNOW where your home is. Your "home" doesn't always have to be where you live. Your home is a place where you can be vulnerable, comfortable, and loved. Home is a place where you're surrounded by those you care about, and those who care about you. Sometimes, you can find your home somewhere you didn't expect you would.

I found my home on March 6, 2012 when I first walked through the doors of Paramus' Care Plus building for the first-ever A.L.L.I.E.S. Support Group meeting.

When I was first presented with the option to attend this group, my reaction was to immediately shut down. I didn't need to go to some therapy group to talk about being a lesbian! Even worse, I might be too shy to talk, and I'd have to sit there listening to other people talk about their sexual orientation.

In the beginning, being a member of this group wasn't even an option for me. It wasn't until after I'd met individually with the woman who would be running the group that I began to consider joining.

Just from our first conversation, I could tell that Jami was one of the greatest people I had ever met and probably would ever meet. Aside from having the same name as me, she made me feel comfortable, and the way she talked so excitedly about the group she was trying to put together made the idea of being there seem glorious. So, I joined.

That first day of group was one I'll never be able to forget. Walking down the seemingly endless hallway toward the tiny room at the end, my hands were shaking and I could feel waves of anxiety drowning out all of my senses. My only clear thoughts were all of the questions whose answers were just behind that door: What would it be like? Would I like anyone there? Would they like me?

Having finally reached the closed door, which was painted in what would soon become my favorite shade of green, I tapped on it softly. A friendly, "Come in!" sounded from inside, and I slowly grabbed the cold doorknob. Taking a deep breath, I opened the door and allowed my feet to walk into the room. Staring back at me were some of the friendliest faces and kindest people that would ever come into my life.

Since that first day, the group has become my biggest support system. I've made friends who have truly changed my life and will continue to change the rest of it. I have connected with inspiring people and have listened to their uplifting stories. I've been able to learn things about myself that I would still be blind to without group. I've made memories. I've found my home.

The A.L.L.I.E.S. group has taught me the importance of stepping out of my comfort zone, giving things a chance, and taking every single one of those crazy opportunities and running with them—because I can never know what might come of them unless I try. Group has taught me how to truly be alive. I know I wouldn't be the same without it.

Find your place—the place you that makes you feel safe and loved, the place where you know you belong the second you walk through the door. Find the place that will allow you to come out of your shell, be yourself, and truly open your heart. Step out of your comfort zone. Go somewhere you never would have, and take a chance. You might end up finding your best friend, your support, or the people who will save your life.

When you find that place, the rest of your world will fall into line. When you find that place, the experiences that will come from it will be limitless. When you find that place, you will be happy ... because you'll be home.

Learning to Love (You)

Ryan Cassata

SOME PEOPLE SAID I HAD MAJOR "BALLS" to do what I did. Coming out on international television to every single person I knew, all at once. The truth was, I didn't have any balls, and I wanted them—that's why I was on TV.

I was ready to liberate the man inside of me and say good-bye to the young girl who was holding me back. I was never really a girl—society just told me that I was. I had tried to stick with that, but my mind was too strong, and I had to come out.

Middle school had been torturous. I first came out as a lesbian, and the kids didn't like that too much. What was even worse was my undying love for the Boston Red Sox. New York middle school kids hated me for it. When Johnny Damon got traded from the Red Sox to a rival team, the clean-cut New York Yankees, kids broke into my locker and hung up newspaper pictures of Johnny Damon's hair being cut.

I would hate going to school if the Red Sox had lost to the Yankees the night before, because I knew my day would be filled with nasty comments. I couldn't handle the anti-Red Sox comments on top of the "he-she," "dyke" and "faggot" comments.

One day, I just couldn't stand middle school anymore, and I broke down before the first-period bell even rang. I wouldn't stop crying, either. The tears just kept on coming. I felt embarrassed and ashamed, and I hated myself.

When an hour had passed and I wouldn't stop crying, my advisor sent me to the school psychologist. "Do you have thoughts of hurting the other students?" Frankly, I was too much of a pacifist for that. I really just wanted to learn and to make friends. The school psychologist continued to question me, and as my answers turned darker and darker, the truth spilled about the scars and slits all over my legs.

When the school nurse made me take my pants off to examine the wounds, I felt more depressed than I had in my entire life. When my dad did the same thing after I got home, my mind turned to complete darkness. I was already drinking liquor, smoking cigarettes, and carrying around a razor blade in my pocket. I was thirteen.

By fourteen, I had unwillingly lost my virginity to someone I thought I could trust. After that incident, sex became my vice, and I fell into more dangerous activities, like hard drinking and soft drugs. My teenage years became darker and darker. I would sneak out of my house late at night and sit on the dock down the street and look at the Great South Bay. With my feet dangling over the edge, I would contemplate my life. I remember how small I felt against the entire bay.

Then one day, I was sitting there with you. And I was screaming at the top of my lungs. And the seagulls were trying so hard to fly above us, but the wind was too strong and they were stuck in midair. And I realized how stuck I was. And I screamed, "I just want to be your boyfriend!" And I came out to you, just like that. And I never looked back.

For a few days, we didn't talk much, because you had to let my new identity into your heart. But you eventually did. I was in love with you and I could feel how intense your love was for me. My identity didn't matter. In that moment, I knew that no matter how I identified, I would always find love.

Love is what keeps me going—the type of love that makes me stop eating and sleeping for a few days as it settles in my stomach. The type of love that makes me travel all the way across the country to chase after someone special. The type of love that my parents expressed when they finally came around and supported my transition. The type of love that my little brother showcased when he stuck up for me when I was too weak to use my own words. The type of love that makes my fans come up to me after a show and tell me that, if I didn't exist, than they wouldn't either.

Then I realized love was everywhere, and it's not even hiding. You just have to love yourself before you can really find it and feel it. And as I began to love myself more and more each day, I began to find love in my everyday life.

Things got easier for me. Things got better for me. I healed my wounded heart, and I kept on going with life. Now, I don't want to ever die. I want to spend each day loving with my whole heart, because it feels that good to love and to be loved.

I've overcome my darkest demons, and thanks to your help and your unconditional love, I learned how to love.

The Bully in Me

Matthew Shaffer

I WAS NINE YEARS OLD the first time I entered a dance studio. The intoxicating smells of ambition, sweat, and leather Capezio jazz oxfords permeated the hardwood floors. (It was the first time in my life that a scent other than food got me excited!)

I stood on the threshold between the carpeted waiting room and the dance floor, which was filled with stunning dancers. Two at a time, they soared through the air with relentless passion. I looked back at my mom and dad and uttered the words that my father had been dying to hear from his only son for soccer, baseball, football or any other sport ending in "ball": "Sign me up!" Without hesitation, my parents enrolled me in Beginning Teen Jazz, and my journey began.

During the first three years of dance, most of my grade school friends had no idea that I spent every Thursday night perfecting my #JazzHands with a room full of girls. By the time I reached middle school, I could no longer hide my enthusiasm. It was not a hobby. I was not "collecting" dance.

Dance was much more significant to me than a sport. I watched my friends play sports, and most of them hated it. I LOVED to dance. I was fully committed to becoming a professional dancer, and I wasn't concerned with anyone else's judgment. Or so I thought.

Everyone who survived junior high knows how devastatingly cruel Tweenagers can be. Nowadays, we use the term bullying—but growing up, it was just my life. At first, the negative comments and painful attacks on my character just stung. I'd seen *Can't Buy Me Love,* so I was prepared for the usual teenage taunting. However, as I continued to pursue dance, the "jokes" turned into torment.

Let me set the stage: I was freakishly short for my age and very round. I wore dress pants from the Macy's "husky" department with vintage, button-down dress shirts from my grandpa's closet. To make matters worse, I had developed a serious case of acne from all of the stress. (Imagine a fabulously styled Mr. Potato Head with a pepperoni pizza face.) So yeah, that was fun.

Several kids spent every lunch period harassing me to the point where I could no longer eat in the cafeteria. Others would follow me between classes shouting "Butterball," "Fatty," "Fag," and other hateful slurs.

I ignored the situation until rumors wound their way through the nasty schoolyard grapevine and into my little sister's ears. She was so devastated by those evil words that I actually considered quitting dance. I begged her not to tell my parents, because I was embarrassed that I was being made fun of. I spent every night crying myself to sleep, praying that the kids would stop tormenting me so that I could keep doing what I loved.

The bullying continued until one day in seventh grade, when the anger and rage boiling inside motivated me to stand up and roar back. (Imagine a clip from *When Animals Attack* on the Discovery Channel.) I was the lone hyena attacking the lions to shreds. Needless to say, from then on, kids avoided me the way an "A-List" actress avoids carbs.

Once I got to high school, I discovered that the kids who harassed me saw something in me that terrified them. They realized I was a confident person working toward a remarkable goal. I wasn't afraid to stand out or be different, and they couldn't control that.

After graduation, I was fully prepared for my life as a sassy, slightly short-statured entertainer with a plenty of personality. Unfortunately, I had not yet realized that the biggest bully I was ever going to encounter was me.

As I set off on my professional career, I convinced myself that the only way I was going to be successful as an actor was if I hid the fact that I was gay. Let's be honest. It's not like Hollywood was embracing "out" actors at the time, and unless you had a body like Matt Bomer or the nerd appeal of Zachary Quinto, Tinseltown isn't exactly celebrating openly gay men in leading roles even now.

I spent my early twenties in the closet, dating girls and acting like a frat brother at every audition. Aside from a small group of friends, with whom I was completely open, I fought every natural instinct to be funny, authentic, or fabulous because of my fear of being discovered. I carefully crafted the way I talked, dressed, and socialized. I bullied myself into believing that who I am wasn't good enough.

When I turned thirty, my grandpa–who was an incredibly supportive figure in my life–told me, just before he passed away, that he was so proud of me for following my dream. Suddenly, it dawned on me that, unlike my seventh-grade self, I had become a victim. I'd spent an entire decade of my adult life pretending to be someone else and it hadn't brought me any closer to my goals.

Finally, I'd reached a point where I was tired of running from myself. I decided that living a truthful life (ironic for an actor) was more important than being famous. Once I gave myself permission to love myself entirely, a universe of unexplored creativity and opportunities emerged.

My partner and I began writing and producing our own digital short sketches, which attracted a huge online fan base. I came out in a national magazine, I wrote and published a book, and I started working as an actor in areas that are perfectly suited to my talents.

More importantly, now I can openly share my story and create work that is grounded in issues and subjects that are relevant to me, hopefully provoking someone else to conquer adversity and triumph on their journey.

The Girl Behind the Mask

Claire Kaufman

EVER SINCE I WAS A LITTLE KID, I was the girl with a smile on her face, laughing till I was on the ground. But by eighth grade, it wasn't real laughter anymore. The smiling took effort. Once I got to high school, it became difficult to even get out of bed in the morning.

To make matters worse, I attended a high school where everyone was overly obsessive about his or her weight, and so ... I felt pressured to stop eating. I also started to come to terms with my sexual orientation—the realization that I am attracted to both males and females, which made me feel even more alienated from my peers.

Depression was taking over my life. It would become so overwhelming that when I would trip and fall, my whole day was ruined. I had plunged into an extremely dark place, and everywhere I turned I felt like someone was saying I wasn't good enough.

{ 179 }

Staying up to date with the trends, constant concerns about weight, being surrounded by the competition for the best grades and extracurricular activities, associating with negative people, and my fear of identifying as queer only had negative impacts on my mental health.

As a result, I transferred to an all-girls Catholic high school that was smaller and less competitive. I was hoping that my issues would disappear if I left the high-pressure environment at my previous school. Things started out okay, but I was ignoring the underlying emotions that had consumed me at my previous school. The more I tried to ignore my negative feelings, the more they escalated. Since I was an amazing masker of my emotions, nobody knew about any of my issues.

I started lying to my friends, family, therapist, and myself, telling everyone that I was fine. My insecurities grew to be unbearable. I thought people felt obligated to spend time with me. In reality, I had a handful of caring people in my life—but I couldn't see that with the dark cloud of depression blinding me.

Negative thoughts and emotions began to consume me, and I eventually became suicidal. Every time I drove by Lake Michigan, I could imagine myself disappearing, hoping I could walk into the water and never be seen again. After a few months of feeling suicidal, I couldn't handle life anymore. I went out to the pool on a sunny summer day and attempted to take my life.

After an hour of attempting to drown in the pool, I gave up. Because of my depression, I had no energy to continue in my attempt to die ... and barely enough of a will to live.

After my suicide attempt, I continued to talk about disappearing into water, and as time passed, everyone agreed that I needed to be admitted to a hospital. I was in the hospital inpatient unit for three weeks, and was then admitted to the outpatient program for a little over a month.

All I wanted to do was get out of the hospital as soon as possible, so I used my amazing masking abilities to get out. Hiding my emotions backfired on me once again, and I ended up back in the hospital. With a good deal of therapy and support from friends and family, life started to improve.

Unfortunately, attending a Catholic high school, I had a hard time justifying that mental health was just as important as physical health. Some of the other students as well as parents and teachers complained about my low attendance during my difficult time. But once I started feeling stronger, I began brainstorming ways to educate my peers about the importance of mental health.

I created a documentary about mental health, which my supportive teachers showed in their classes. After showing this video in a few classes, a student told me that I had helped save her life. She thanked me for encouraging her to reach out for help. That moment was life-changing for me. It encouraged me to become a lifelong advocate for suicide prevention.

After my senior year of high school, I started to walk in the American Foundation for Suicide Prevention's (AFSP) Out of the Darkness Overnight Walks. I attended my first Out of the Darkness Overnight walk in Chicago, and I realized how empowering and important that walk was for those battling mental illness, and for those who have lost loved ones.

The next year, I signed up for the Boston Out of the Darkness Overnight Walk. After the Boston walk, I felt mentally stronger than ever before and ready to bring suicide prevention awareness to my own community.

Once I started attending the University of Wisconsin at Madison, I gathered a handful of passionate students to join me in planning the First Annual Out of the Darkness Campus Walk. Our walk was not just a success in Wisconsin, but it was the most successful suicide-prevention campus walk in the nation.

The journey from having no energy to get out of bed, all the way to gathering a large group of students to plan the most successful Out of the Darkness Campus Walk in the country, has been an extremely rewarding experience. Now in my last semester of college, I'm feeling stronger than ever. I am ready to enter the real world with all the strength I have built through my activist work, supportive friends and family, and my spirit of perseverance.

Making it Big

James Lecesne

YOU WILL NEVER MAKE IT," the man says.

"Not big, not in this business."

Though what business it was of his, I can't recall.

His name?

His name was ...

His name is gone.

But his words burned, tattoo-like, into my brain.

"No, you will not make it big.

And do you know how I know this?" he asks me.

And I say, "No, no, I don't know." Noting that I say *no* twice in the same breath.

And that can't be good. No, no. As though something deep down in me doesn't really want to know. But never mind, here he goes, he's on a roll, the man.

"Because," he says, "you are too gay."

And that gay word slices clean through me like a bullet through butter.
But hey, I grew up with people saying worse than gay to me.
They raised fists, sticks, and once a boot to make their point.
They called me faggot, sissy, girly boy—and that was just to get my attention.

"I hate to say it," the man says, in that way that some people just love to say, "but ...
Gay will get you nowhere.
Gay is your Achilles heel.
Gay is not the universal formula for success."
And just like that, I'm done for, discarded, plucked from the running and transformed into a common loser, without my say-so.

So I say, "Fine.
But let me get this straight.
Are you suggesting that in order to succeed, I will have to be less gay?"
"No," he says, "that's my point. You? You couldn't be less gay if you tried."
And then, in a manner that astounds me to remember even now, the words tumbling from my twenty-something-year-old mouth, I tell the man, "Well, then I guess I'll have to change my definition of success."

This will not be the last time that it happens.
Others will come along offering sidelong glances and outright statements;
They will be there at every turn, reminding me
to tone it down,

butch it up,

watch my back,

don't dance so much,

gesture less,

lose the lisp,

straighten up,

buckle down,

wear a tie,

don't be such a girl.

In short, they will want me to be less myself—

as if such a thing were possible.

A New York agent will kindly agree to represent me as an actor, but not before he offers this: "Are you aware that you come off a little gay?"

A little?

Yes, I will tell him, and then I walk out of that office, head held high—

but his word will bang in my ear for years. "A little gay."

It's faggot, sissy, girly-boy all over again.

A woman with a big desk will caution me about the dangers of declaring myself.

She will list the casualties, recount the missteps of others in the business of show who showed too much, dared to say, went that way, were themselves.

Then she'll end her speech by saying: "In this town, if you want to live by the sword, you must die by the sword."

I will get the point.

It's the raised fist, the big stick, the boot—all over again.

Others will be subtler.

But it won't just be the showbiz folks who flick an eye or quick-clear their throats to keep me close in check. Everyone will try to rein me in, shut me down, signal me to just get over it, already—as if such a thing were possible.

It will go on like this for years.
And yet, despite how hard they try,
Despite the many warnings, threats, prizes, perks
They offer me to be something other than my Self,
I will never stop.
It just won't happen.
Turns out, people come and go.
Self sticks true.

Now that I am so much more my Self, I know that making it big
Means making more and more myself.
Making it big means expanding self to include everything skin-out, the whole damn world, in fact. Can I make it mine?
You too. Yes, even you.
Whether you are lesbian, gay, bi, transgender, cisgendered, two spirit, androgyne, questioning, queer, intersex, asexual, pansexual, hetero, or just some undeclared freelance super hero on the fly, can I make you mine?
Is there room enough in me for you?
Is there love enough?

Can I convince each and every one of you that, though I am standing here, right here—and you are there, right there—together WE are the universal formula for success.
And that—

That togetherness is what works and is
What allows us all to stand and, in one voice, say to the Man:
Please, step it back a bit so you can see what's what and what
It looks like to, yes, yes, truly make it big.

Second Acts and Second Chances

"Look on every exit as being an entrance somewhere else."
  - Tom Stoppard

13

Just Pray for that Upper Right Hook

Brent Buell

MORE YEARS AGO than I would ever disclose (even if Dick Cheney's "friends" were treating me to the water-board experience), I was sitting in my parents' living room tearfully imploring them to listen to me. "Mom, Dad, the one thing I want to do in life is to act, write novels, and make movies!"

"But fiction, theater, and motion pictures are tools of the Devil, and you'll be playing into Satan's hands if you go where your guardian angel can't go with you."

I suppose my groans are still reverberating in that Orange County, California room all these (undisclosed number of) years later. I was twelve years old. The future—an endless parade of church potlucks and gospel-approved professions (minister, minister, or minister) lay ahead of me.

I tried running away from home a number of times—once with a carnival, once with the Ice Follies, and once just over the back fence—but inevitably, I was discovered, captured, and returned to what was declared to be the "service of God."

I would succumb to the pressure and make a show of "rededicating" myself to the church. But while that cycle repeated itself for years, inside I knew that there was only one future for me: writing and the theater.

I entered college as a reluctant theology major and dedicated myself tirelessly to the study of ancient Greek, Biblical history, and scriptural discourse ... for nearly three weeks. I think a major turning point was when, while I was sitting in the front row of my 6:30 a.m. religion class, I fell asleep and dreamed I was skiing and about to hit a tree. I leapt to my feet, screaming, "Oh ... my ... God!"

It was the most religious statement I would make during my entire college education—so it seemed positive. But after my cry to my Creator was rebuked by the professor, I knew I had to get myself connected with the godless theater people and novelists who would understand me.

Years passed. By this time, I was doing some writing and at least associating with a lot of actors. I had just gone through a horrendous divorce and was inevitably hearing, "Your life is in the mess it's in now because you have turned from the Truth and are indulging in satanic pursuits (those were some short stories that, while quite harmless, were nevertheless fiction).

I was incredibly depressed, and even though I still dreamed of novels, theater, and film, I was still influenced enough by family pressures that their condemnation became mingled with my own fears—and I was at a standstill.

One night, I was visiting a friend on his houseboat and in my most dramatic, two-beers-induced confessional tones, I exclaimed, "I think I'm going crazy."

My friend was a no-nonsense guy who later went on to become a county sheriff in Northern California. He liked me, but he thought my theatricality should be making me money, not getting his houseboat flooded with tears. He walked over to me, pulled back his fist, and clocked me with an upper right hook that knocked me across the room.

"Don't you EVER say anything like that again," he screamed. "You're one of the strongest people I know. Now get yourself together and go after what you know you ought to be doing!"

I don't remember if I thanked him or not. In fact, I don't remember much of the rest of that evening. But by the next day, I know I felt like ducking every time a negative thought came into my head.

A few weeks later, a friend called and asked if I would like to move to New York. I jumped at the chance and landed a job managing a famous Manhattan nightclub that catered to Broadway show people. It was there that my career got a jumpstart.

So where am I going with this? Just this: About the time you think that every roadblock in front of you has been made of reinforced concrete, and when you're being scolded and harassed by the people you've known—just when you think that not only has the bottom fallen out, but that the roof has caved in, too—that's the time to look for that upper right hook that the universe sends you. It says, "What was in your heart all along was *right*—now pick up your self-loathing behind and go after your dreams."

I got my upper right hook—the actual one and some more as I started writing and acting—but because of what I had learned, they propelled me forward, not backward.

Today, as an actor with some nice credits, as a director who's currently working Off Broadway, and as a theater producer of a major, upcoming hip-hop musical, I really can say that just when things look the worst is when they start to get better.

Oh, and about those forbidden novels? My novel, *RAPTUROUS*— an action-adventure that looks at politics and religion from a unique angle—is currently selling internationally.

And guess what? Before my dad passed, a number of years ago, he came to New York and saw me performing. He went home and bragged about me to all his friends. I guess, in pursuing my dream, I also chased Satan away.

The 4th Book of Dave
David Nathan Scott

CHAPTER I - DAVE RECEIVES BAD NEWS

1. It came to pass in the year two thousand and twelve, during the beginning of the summer, that the Spirit of the Lord came to Dave, a struggling musician, and said, "You must leave New York City, for I have closed its doors to you. Thou art behind on your rent. This city will no longer provide you with work. I have even smitten your auditions from Craigslist."

2. Dave was filled with fear, humiliation, and devastation. On a bench overlooking the Hudson River, he wondered if he had the courage to start over yet again and contemplated inviting the depths of the Hudson into his lungs.

3. And Dave said to the Spirit, "Why would you drive me from the life I know and send me off into the unknown? Have I not suffered enough? After all, is it not said, "If you can make it here, you can make it anywhere"?

4. Spirit spoke and said, "Here is wherever you are. Now put your possessions in order, for you will be going to live with your brother. There your spirit will refresh and you will create a new life."

5. Unable to afford to travel by air, Dave left the city that had been his home stealthily in the night, by Greyhound. With the exception of three chosen people, no one knew he had left. "It will be like going on tour," he said to those chosen few. For though he could not say it aloud, he felt ashamed.

6. As he traveled the thousand miles to his destination, he relived his recent past. He had been a wealthy man for six of the last eight years. But he had not heeded those that had warned him of the dangers of unbridled generosity. He had given to the point of financial ruin, had seen the abyss beckoning, and had painfully made his way into her center with stoic resignation—all but homeless.

CHAPTER II – DAVE IS GIVEN A GIFT

1. Dave felt as if he were in a dream. As if he had been ripped from one movie and deposited in another. Although many times he had visited and stayed with his family—this was different. He had now, in some way, become prisoner to the very environment he had run away from years before. He missed his friends, especially his young friend J-Rivs. They had bonded in theatre, good conversation, and travels. And now they were a thousand miles apart.

2. His brother Joey welcomed him, and immediately seemed glad that he would now have company. "I put a circular about employment opportunities on the table for you," Joey would say, "and UPS wouldn't be such a bad job." Although he never said

it, Dave thought, "I'd rather die than be relegated to employ-ment designed to suck the life out of a human being. I am going to sing for my supper."

3. Then the Spirit of the Lord came to him and said, "I will give you music in abundance—in the belly of a computer hard drive. This will give you confidence to speak on your behalf and seek gigs." And Dave said, "Awesome. Really awesome. Thank you."

4. And the Spirit of the Lord gave unto Dave many songs, in many styles and genres. No. Really. He gave him backing tracks to a heck of a lot of music.

5. Dave immediately began to reach out to those who were shut in and infirm, and offered to share with them his voice and music for an agreed upon sum in the form of *The David Nathan Scott Show*. He left many messages, oftentimes calling three and four times, and still not reaching a prospective employer. But he did not give up.

6. As he waited for someone to hire him, Dave booked a small movie gig and made his first dollars in this foreign land. This provided the means to purchase the equipment necessary to perform: PA system, percussion, cables, and microphones.

CHAPTER III – DAVE FINDS HOPE

1. It came to pass after a month that a woman said to him, "Yes, you can come sing for us. If they like you, we will book you every month. But I cannot pay what you ask. Will you do it for less?" And Dave said, "Yes."

2. The residents of Magnolia House loved him. They were thrilled to see him every month. They would do their hair,

give him homemade cards and presents, and shower him with hugs and appreciation.

3. Other places began to hire him. Many also gave him a permanent date every month, and the residents would pound their hearts and shout, "We love you!" or "Don't forget to come back" or "You can come every day if you want." He was given flowers, teddy bears, and money was pressed into his hand.

4. Administrators, staff, and family also came up to Dave, and said "Thank you." Many of them recommended him to other places, where he also was well-received. Much joy and dancing followed wherever he went.

5. Soon Dave found a version of life he had never known before. He was able to use his heart and talent to survive. He began to find time and means to travel and experience both new and familiar places, many of them with his good friend J-Rivs. He made new friends and renewed old ones in his adopted homeland, and he found himself surrounded by those who loved him and aided and abetted his talents.

6. And Dave said to Spirit, "I feel closer to you than I ever have before. Through all my mistakes and shortcomings, I am living my fantasy. Though it is for hundreds, not hundreds of thousands, I am sharing all my love, and I am sharing you." And Spirit said, "Right on."

i

All In

Kenny Medrano

YOU LEARNED A WEEK EARLIER your teacher had decided not to press charges.

You were awaiting a call from the principal about your fate.

It was right before the end of the school year.

Then came the turning point of your life.

Your mom received the call.

The principal explained you were officially expelled from school.

Your mom hung up.

Her arms were flailing to hit you and she began to cry so hard that it just became an empty scream; she collapsed.

You thought she was having a stroke.

You knelt down to her and apologized over and over, and in that moment, all she could utter was "How could you do this to us?"

That's when it hit you.

You let her down.

You, her only child, who was an honor roll student all throughout school, officially became a kid with *no* school.

You felt the emptiness of having no place to go.

You'd been drinking since you were twelve years old, but no amount of beer could have filled up the emptiness you felt after she got that call from the principal.

Your mom, a janitor who lost her job after 9/11, woke up every single morning at 5 a.m. to call and see if there was work for that day.

You were tired of hearing those sighs of disappointment every time there wasn't work.

Your mom sacrificed so much in her life so you could be her ticket to a better one.

Instead, you became her biggest disappointment.

It felt like the only person who truly loved you was giving up on you … and that made you want to give up on yourself.

The place you were in was your lowest of lows, both mentally and spiritually.

Rejected, abandoned, and experiencing your biggest fear of all: you were not worth being loved.

But the world was not to blame.

You put *yourself* in this corner, and all you had was yourself to rely on.

You got what you wanted.

But this wasn't just you against the world.

You had someone to look after as well: your mom.

That's when you had a moment of clarity.

You were confronted by two decisions:

You either take a route toward self-destruction, while hurting the person closest to you,

OR

You take the route toward redemption, while being a person your mom can rely on.

You chose the latter, and you put in the work.

You wrote poems and essays with the hope that, if you explained your new sense of enlightenment, schools would accept you.
They didn't. You refused to accept that, so you kept trying.
The school year had started and you still had nowhere to go.
It now seemed as if your only option was to live with your half-sister in Long Island.
In turn, you would have to leave everything behind, including your mother.

And then: serendipity.
That first week in September, you were speaking with an acquaintance, Andy, from your former school.
He got expelled, just like you.
In that conversation, he told you how he had applied to and was now entering a school in Queens.
He recommended you contact them.
You did …
… and you were accepted.

You had one goal in mind:
To graduate.
This was now your third school in three years, and you weren't going to let a second chance to redeem yourself slip away.
You were unconcerned with making new friends. Andy, your acquaintance, was the only friend you had in that school.

You had the best academic year of your high school life.

You took job employment sessions.

You received an offer to work in an after-school program.

You gave twenty percent of your check to your mom and asked her to use it to help pay rent.

You went back to church, hoping to fill the spiritual void inside.

These were your first steps, after years, to confront the conflicts of your soul.

You realized, sometimes greatness comes out of even the darkest of moments.

You went through other major hurdles of this magnitude, but you know what?

You realized you were less fearful.

How could there be fear?

You had been at the lowest you could go, and you rose to the occasion.

You embraced the pressure, you put up a fight, you gave it your all, and you became a better person after that.

In this game of life, your approach is to try your hardest to conquer every fear in your way so you can ultimately win.

In tackling these fears, you begin to increase your self-worth, and you start realizing that you are worth being loved.

You now let your mind transform the negative into a positive.

Now you have the confidence to do *anything* you set your mind to.

It's all a journey, and you're happy you made a conscious decision for positive change.

All that pain, hurt, struggle, and depression in your life, past and present, was there to create the strength to power through and persist in a lifelong pursuit of happiness.

You told yourself you would never write this.

You didn't trust anyone.

All these years, you held on to these secrets and this pain because you were building a wall to imprison yourself.

You told yourself, who on Earth could possibly understand what you went through?

Until today.

Today is the day you chose to write.

Now, you can finally let your guard down.

You realize that you didn't just write this for yourself.

You wrote this for others who are feeling at their very lowest.

You wrote this piece to let them know they can *always* redeem themselves.

Because when it's all said and done, when you've already hit your lowest, what do you have to lose?

Go all in.

Kat's Second Lease on Life

Kathleen Myre

N 2000, MY HUSBAND and I purchased our first home in New Jersey. It wasn't our dream house, but it was in our price range and had three bedrooms—one for my husband and me, and one each for our daughter and infant son.

As our children grew, I went from having everyday Mom-worries to full-blown anxiety. I worried that we would not be able to provide for our children. I questioned whether we were raising them properly and wondered if our actions were always in their best interest.

During the summer of 2004, while we were at our summer getaway, there were signs that all was not well with me—but I just walked around smiling, pretending I was fine. My husband knew I had constant migraines and knots in my shoulders and neck, but he didn't know about the battle taking place in my head, the voice that kept telling me I was a loser and a failure, and that one day I would lose the love of not only my husband, but also my children. I was miserable, but I reasoned that the feelings would pass, that the voice would go away, and that all would be well again.

But those summer symptoms did not go away. That fall, my body completely shut down. I was sleeping all day, crying incessantly, and vomiting when I tried to eat. I needed help, but pride and stubbornness kept me from admitting it, even to my husband, until one November day when I could hide it no more. An extensive emergency room visit confirmed that I was in the throes of clinical depression and also suffering from anxiety-related issues.

When I finally found the right psychiatrist, the right therapist, and the right treatment plan, I felt as though I had hit the lottery. I discovered that the coping skills I had developed as a child were no match for this battle. I needed to work on myself and the way I responded to the world around me. I slowly began to regain my life. The happy days with my husband and children, which I had convinced myself I would never experience again, returned.

The most difficult lesson for me during my recovery was that I needed to put myself first. Doing so wasn't being selfish, but absolutely vital to my recovery. I am thankful for my depression experience, because I not only learned from it, but flourished as a result of it.

I still continue to face challenges, but I now understand they are a part of life and that I am responsible for how I face them. One challenge I am currently addressing is speaking publicly about my depression, as opposed to keeping it under lock and key for fear of being judged or, even worse, pitied.

On April 24, 2013, I learned that sharing my depression experience could help others and possibly save lives. I had attended a performance at a local college and was captivated by the performer's openness and honesty as he told his story. He changed me and my outlook on life and depression for the better that day, and I hope that I can inspire others as much as he has inspired me.

If you feel or think you are depressed, find someone you can trust and confide what has been going on in your life. The fears that prevent you from speaking up and seeking help are only feasting upon you and weighing you down. You are not alone, you are not helpless, and you are not weak. It is strong and brave to open yourself up to someone and ask for help. It is the first step on your journey to recovery.

i

·······································

Doorsteps
Nancy Tetreaux

I DON'T REMEMBER HOW IT ALL STARTED, but stacks of letters from animal shelters began showing up in my mail. At first they were just from local places, but in a matter of months, it seemed like every animal rescue organization in the Northern hemisphere had my name and address.

This was back in the days when all mail was paper. I'd stand at my kitchen counter opening one sad letter after another—one from the neighborhood shelter for dogs and cats, one from the Southwest for abused horses, one from the Northwest for endangered birds—and pleas to help elephants, whales, lions, dolphins, chimpanzees, circus animals, lab animals, and forest animals. All beautiful, innocent animals.

I had been at least somewhat aware of the plight of animals before this onslaught of mail, if only from hearsay. Years earlier, a friend in the medical field had told me about how pharmaceutical and cosmetic companies tested their products on animals. She had shown me pictures taken in laboratories, and they were horrifying.

Though I didn't *have to* read all those letters to know that millions of animals were suffering every moment of every day, I read them anyway. I felt like it was my responsibility. And the stories devastated me.

At this time in my life, I was unhappily married. My ex-husband was a troubled soul who was big on insults. In profound and little ways, his words and behavior wore away at my confidence and self-esteem. Whether it was my intelligence, my appearance, or my personality, on any given day, he managed to find something terribly wrong with me. He would criticize me one day, and then tell me the next day that he didn't mean it, and then tell me on yet another day that he really *did* mean it and he had just been trying to make me feel better when he had said he *didn't* mean it.

I came to dread going home at the end of the day, but I felt overwhelmed by the thought of leaving to start a new life on my own. I was becoming immobilized by despair.

Trying to figure out what to do, I sought the guidance of a therapist, Alice. Over the course of several months, I discussed with Alice the usual therapy topics: childhood stuff and my feelings about it, my dreams, and my life in general. Eventually, I described my "animal mail" to Alice, and how I dutifully read all of it, day after day. I described my worry over so many animals suffering in the world, and my incapacity to help them all. I told her it was keeping me awake at night.

In Alice's opinion, I not only felt sorry for these animals as any animal-lover would, but due to my difficulties at home, I was identifying with them. She believed that I was confusing my own feelings of sadness and fear with those I attributed to the animals in my mail.

At first, I rejected this notion. I thought I was perfectly able to separate my thoughts about my own life from those about these sad animals. But the more I thought about it, the more I came to see that Alice was right. The steady stream of words and images of animals in distress stoked my own sense of helplessness. They seemed so alone in the world, and so did I.

Alice gently insisted I stop reading my animal mail. "Throw it away without looking at it for the next few weeks, and see how you feel," she said. And so I did—guiltily at first. But then a gentle wave of relief began to wash over my mind. I was able to sleep better and think more clearly.

I realized that I needed to take better care of myself. "One hand for the ship, one hand for yourself," my father used to say when he saw me committing to too many things at once. I made a commitment to myself to regain my strength. Once I had done that, I would figure out how to help the animals.

* * *

In the late '80s and early '90s, I read many books on Native American religion and philosophy, which were popular at that time. Among them was a book about the Cherokee Medicine Man, Rolling Thunder. Around the time I had given up reading my animal mail, I happened upon an idea in this book that has served me well ever since.

Essentially, Rolling Thunder taught that each of us must care for the world we find at our doorsteps—the people, the Earth, and her plants and animals. Few of us have the capacity to protect and relieve the suffering of Nature far and wide, but we all have the responsibility to do what we can for the Nature we live with, and in, day-to-day. Doing what we can is not only good enough—it is as it should be.

I made a decision to do as much for the animals as I could without over-extending myself. I chose a handful of organizations to which I contributed my money and time. And I would get out of my marriage and get on with my life. Early one spring morning, after my husband went to work, I packed a shopping bag and left for good. A few months later, I filed for a divorce.

It was Ghandi who said, "The greatness of a nation and its moral progress can be judged by the ways its animals are treated." Do unto others—Nature and her animals included—as we would have done unto ourselves. If we all did this, the patchwork of our doorsteps would cover the Earth.

My own healing occurred when I realized I couldn't help others unless I helped myself first. How many we help matters less than helping those we can—including ourselves.

My Mother Was a Con Artist

Carlo D'Amore

M Y MOTHER WAS A CON ARTIST—there is no shame it that, it's just a fact. And I do say she *was*, as in the past, like she no longer is a con artist. And that is what makes this an extraordinary story.

My mother was a full-fledged criminal with an extensive and impressive list of crimes that started with shoplifting and extended to pen and paper crimes like forgery, and then progressed into larceny, grand theft, embezzlement, drug trafficking, stealing drugs from drug dealers, huge immigration scams … and the list goes on.

For close to forty years, my mother did things that were "wrong" on a very simplistic level—but she was my mother, and I was her closest confidant, and many times over an accomplice to her crimes. As a young child I would look out for her as she stole *haute couture* articles from high-end stores, and I peed my pants for years from the trauma. I would play the dutiful child dressed in my Sunday best, sitting in the front row of many a courtroom with well-orchestrated tears streaming down my face.

It was incredibly confusing as a child, because I adored and worshipped my mother, as she did me, and I bathed in the comforts that she provided most willingly. By the time I was eighteen, I had gone through my very own convertible Fiat Spider, a brand new Honda Prelude, and a fantastic Dodge Bronco, as well as a cutting edge Saab. My tag (or nickname) in high school was "Cashflow."

Even though we had everything, my mother's actions created total and earth-shattering chaos within our family. She was finally sentenced to ten years in prison. On the day of her release, she was deported back to her native country. But always the con, she snuck back in a few years later—because nothing would keep her away from her family.

Once back in the U.S., she began conning again, because, "Prison doesn't work. It only teaches you how to be better at what you do," as she so aptly put it. But with her re-entry into conning, it wasn't the police that caught up to her this time, but a debilitating stroke.

I was living across the country at the time—apparently not far enough away to avoid being sucked into the cyclone of havoc wreaked by my mother. I was called in to rescue her by providing her with a refuge from the law. I made up all kinds of excuses as to why I couldn't have her living with me, but my sense of duty to her and family made me cave in.

She moved in with me to my fifth floor walk-up on the Lower East Side of Manhattan. There I was, a struggling actor saddled with the responsibility of taking care of my stroked out, con artist mother. But I'm nothing if not adaptable to change. My mother had taught me well.

So I began to take care of her, and slowly, she became her old self. She even pulled a couple of scams on me—little things, but to me, they were the last straw in this almost-forty-year ordeal.

I did the only thing I could: I punished her. I meant business, and the only way I could punish her was to stop talking to her.

The silent treatment took its toll. Every night I could hear her whimpering herself to sleep. On Silent Treatment Day Number 487—okay, Day Nine—I was in the kitchen quietly picking at a cold empanada. After I wiped my mouth with the paper napkin she had so carefully folded into a little triangle, as she always had, I ran into it. That word: "Mama." And my silence was broken.

What transpired then could only have happened in the way it all had to happen—after her stroke, which in my mind was God's way of dimming her a bit. She had to be under my care, under my roof, and the act of me not talking to her—such a simple act—had profound consequences. For the first time in her life, she admitted wrongdoing. "You mean that I use my intelligence to do bad things," she said. From that moment on, she stopped—never again to do anything criminally minded. It has been eight years, and I guess I might be heartbroken to find out some time in the future that she has started up again, but I don't think I will. So when people say "people don't change" I like to think … people do change, when they choose to change.

** *Some of this text has been adapted from Carlo D'Amore's one-man play* No Parole

Learning to Lead

Camilla Ross

F HINDSIGHT IS SEEN with 20/20 vision, then learning to walk with my left foot first was one of the first clues as to who I would become later in my life. To paraphrase Dorothy Law Nolte, "Children live what they learn."

Growing up, I learned that self-esteem was for those who looked different than me, and that "stupid" was the new word I would live with well into my adult years. I taught myself to become invisible. I became a scholar in all that love was not.

So what sowed the seeds of change? Two words—Basic Training. It wasn't the first time I went to Basic Training (first the Army, then the Navy) but it was a monumental event that changed the direction of where my life was headed. Learning to lead in basic training became my saving grace.

I was young and afraid of failure, but my company commanders saw something in me that I didn't even know existed. They saw a leader—a raw, young woman who was prepared for the task but who lacked commitment to herself. During the second week of training, I was tasked with learning to lead the recruits in training. I was desperately trying to find the right balance. It was a challenging time filled with ups and downs.

Each day changed into the next, and learning to march recruits and call cadence was the order of the day. I mustered up the courage to lead another day, and I did well, in spite of the mistakes. But the company commanders kept the pace and set the standard. Each day, I grew more comfortable in my role, but I had not mastered the ability to love me enough to not care about what others thought. All it took to unravel that confidence I was building was one ill word from a recruit.

"You sound like a man when you call cadence," one female recruit said. And that sent my world into a spiral that I couldn't recover from.

I dropped the baton—in civilian speak, I resigned from my position—and after Week Three, I settled into being second in command of my company. The easy part of leading the recruits lay within my physical strength. I could run farther and do more push-ups than any of the recruits. But I wasn't mentally strong. I had always lived by the lessons planted within me at an early age, to believe what others had said about me. It was difficult to create a new mindset that was free from the outside voices and nasty critics.

After completing basic training, I craved the opportunity to lead, but the fear of failing in the eyes of others weighed heavily upon me and curbed my desire. The biggest obstacle in my life existed only in my head: self-doubt in my many talents and abilities. I had to gradually learn to lead myself out of my own way so that I could grow—one of the many lessons I learned from that experience in basic training. I even learned how to clean floors with a toothbrush (Ha!)

It wasn't until 2008, nineteen years after basic training, when I started my company—the Emerson Theater Collaborative—that I was able to pick up the baton once again and lead with confidence.

Having faith was one thing, but learning to rely and lean on it was another lesson entirely. I had to learn to love and lead myself first before I could lead others. Learning to love myself took time, patience, and self-compassion. It took time to rebuild what others had torn down.

Today, I am able stand on the rock of my childhood and look back and smile. I smile because that child that I was has been renewed in the spirit of my work that I do today.

I am a DIVA! (Dependable, Intelligent, Vivacious and Adaptable) This is the love that I instill in my young girls today. I teach them that loving who you are and where you are in your process is the most important thing. Worry not about what others may say, but look in the mirror and love that person looking back at you.

My accomplishments today are many. I am leading and growing in so many directions that I have to stop, breathe for a moment, and take it all in. I love me.

In 2013, much to my astonishment, I found myself in a beautiful position: I was nominated for Woman of the Year by the Southeastern Connecticut Women's Network, an honor that humbles me to this day. I had to see myself as a leader before I could become one. Does that sound familiar? Being something before you actually are—seeing it *is* believing it.

i'

....

Your i'Mpossible Story

(You)

Author Biographies

Kevin Hines is a mental health advocate, award-winning global speaker, bestselling author, and documentary filmmaker who reaches audiences with his story of an unlikely survival and his strong will to live. Two years after he was diagnosed with bipolar disorder, he attempted to take his life by jumping from the Golden Gate Bridge. Today, Kevin dedicates his life to spreading his message of hope and sharing his art of living mentally well. Kevin's story is a testament to the strength of the human spirit and a reminder for us to love the life we have. www.kevinhinesstory.com

Suzanne Bachner is an award-winning writer and director based in New York City. Her play, *Circle*, ran for five months Off Broadway, was called "ingenious" by The New York Times and completed a four-month, seven-city sold-out international tour during the summer of 2013, winning Most Daring Show of the London Fringe. She is a member of the Dramatists Guild and the United Solo Academy. www.jmtcinc.com

Nikki MacCallum holds a B.M. from New York University. In 2011, MacCallum won the MAC nomination for her writing and performance of her New York City cabaret debut show, *Matchmaker Matchmaker I'm Willing to Settle!*, which has since had full productions at Ars Nova, MGR Playhouse and N.Y.U. She recently finished

26.2, a coming of age memoir that parallels running a marathon with the struggles of an alcoholic parent.

Carl Ballenas comes from a family of healers. His father, Dr. Carlos Ballenas Laos, was a noted gynecologist, surgeon, and teacher; his mother, Lucy Ballenas Guzman, was a midwife; his brother, Dr. Edgar Ballenas, is an Emergency Room physician; and his sister, Dr. Nancy Baxter, is a pediatrician. Carl is an educator who always knew he wanted to be a teacher. His main area of expertise is History. He believes that the greatest natural resource in our country is children. They need to be nurtured in mind and soul.

Jessie Fahay is a published author and playwright—winning the New Jersey Governor's award for one of her original written works. She recently earned an MBA. She has also spent years acting in New York with numerous touring and not-for-profit theatre companies along with being cast in several television/film roles. Her performing experience, her passion for making a difference, her business education, and her experience traveling around the country as a public speaker inspired her to co-found Ripple Effect Artists in 2009.

Mary C. Harris is a free-spirited, nature- and travel-loving individual who has a soft spot in her heart for animals, small houses, and living simply. She lives in New Jersey with her husband Cody and their baby son. Mary is a full-time college professor, a certified holistic health coach, and the volunteer director of an educational vegan/vegetarian nonprofit organization. You can connect with her through her healthy living blog, sproutandblossomwellness.com.

Kelly Wilson is a coach, mentor, trainer, and mom to four children with special needs. Her speciality is in bringing the knowledge from research and effectively implementing it in practice—bridging the gap between research and practice.

Elaine Taylor-Klaus, CPCC, PCC is the co-founder of ImpactADHD.com, an international resource helping parents raise confident, successful children with ADD/ADHD and related challenges. A writer, parenting coach, and public speaker, Elaine is a contributing blogger for the Huffington Post, national Board Member of CHADD (Children and Adults with ADHD), parents representative for the American Academy of Pediatrics, and the mother in an ADHD Family of five.

Natalie Roy was born and raised in Keswick Ridge, New Brunswick, Canada and now lives in New York City. Natalie is an actor who has worked across North America in feature film, television, and on stage. As a writer, her first book, *30. 30 Years. 30 Lessons* was published in 2012. She is also a passionate teacher of creative and spiritual workshops. Natalie dreams of sharing her passion and talents in service to a more inspired and connected world.

Mariagrazia Buttitta was born and raised in Sicily. She was born with a rare eye condition, Cone Dystrophy. She is also combating an anxiety and depressive disorder. In 2013, after seeing a performance that changed her life—*Kicking My Blue Genes in the Butt*—she opened up about her struggles and sought treatment for the first time. Her dream is to become an advocate for both mental health and disabilities, spreading hope and helping others embrace their differences. She loves hiking, writing, and hanging out with her therapy dogs, family, and friends.

Malini Singh McDonald is a native New Yorker. She earned her BA in Theatre Arts and English Literature from Baruch College and her MFA in Directing from the Actors Studio Drama School. Malini's greatest personal achievement was in March 2015 when she climbed sixty-six flights of the Rockefeller Center for the National MS Society of NYC. She is recognized as an Elite 66 for her fundraising efforts. She also recently completed an industrial about living with Multiple Sclerosis.

Ali Stroker was a finalist on Season Two of *The Glee Project* and then played Artie's love interest on the fifth season of *Glee*. She is a graduate of New York University and the first person in a wheelchair to graduate from Tisch's drama program. Ali has been performing on stage and screen since she was seven years old. Her favorite role on stage is "Anna" in Deaf West's *Spring Awakening*. Ali guest stars on MTV's *Faking It*. Ali currently lives in LA. www.alistroker.com

Joe Narciso is a writer and an actor in film, television, theater, and voiceover. www.JoeNarciso.com

Holly Bertone, PMP is an author, blogger, and breast cancer survivor and advocate. She is the president and CEO of Pink Fortitude, LLC and editor-in-chief at the inspirational blog The Coconut Head's Survival Guide. Holly holds a master's degree from Johns Hopkins University, a Bachelor's Degree from Elizabethtown College, and is a Project Management Professional (PMP). Holly is an Ambassador for the Tigerlily Foundation. She was named a 2014 Woman of the Year by the National Association of Professional Women. Holly is married to a retired Green Beret, is a stepmother, and lives in Alexandria, VA.

Evita Ochel is a consciousness-expansion teacher who lives by being the change she wishes to see. Her diverse passions and expertise include being a writer, speaker, holistic nutritionist, web TV host, and author of the book *Healing & Prevention Through Nutrition*. To learn more about her or her work, visit EvitaOchel.com

Julie Ryan is a freelance writer, and maintains her own blog, Counting My Spoons. She lives with a growing list of chronic illnesses that include fibromyalgia, TMJ, chronic migraines, cluster headaches, and endometriosis. Her goal is to inspire and inform others living with chronic illness, to remind them that there is still a life worth living, despite the pain. www.countingmyspoons.com

Barby Ingle is a chronic pain educator, patient advocate, and president of the board for the Power of Pain Foundation. Barby is also a motivational speaker and best-selling author on pain topics. She has been a pain patient since developing endometriosis in 1997 and reflex sympathetic dystrophy in 2002. www.barbyingle.com www.powerofpain.org

Megan Starshak lives in Milwaukee with her dog and boyfriend, and when she's not working on projects in the IBD space, she has a career in marketing. She loves trying new things, which has resulted in too many hobbies such as running, cycling, hiking, photography, archery, and even crocheting.

Suzanne Paire resides in Nether Providence, Pennsylvania with her husband, Paul, and four children. She holds degrees in the field of education from Millersville University and Cabrini College. She has written on a myriad of topics for Examiner.com, edited two books, and is penning one of her own entitled, *The Things Kids Say*. Of her other accomplishments, she can claim All-American athletic honors and giving birth to triplets and their big brother, Tim.

Jane Beller has lived and worked as an actress in LA, Paris, San Francisco, and New York. Seen on stage, screen, and behind a thousand microphones, her favorite voiceover job was the thrill of simply saying: "This is PBS." She is equally thrilled to be part of this meaningful project.

Dana Kukin recently graduated from Barnard College of Columbia University with a degree in Psychology. Dana is the founder of the Columbia/Barnard Hillel Mental Health Awareness Month, now a year-round group known as Nefesh.

Jenny Rietveld is mother and a grandmother. She worked in sales for many years. After retiring, she volunteered in soup kitchens and spent eight years volunteering in palliative care. She loves traveling, history, and reading. She believes in world peace and believes we all need to do more for mental health and suicide prevention in school and in the work place.

Rachel Brummert is the President and Executive Director of the Quinolone Vigilance Foundation. www.SaferPills.org, a nonprofit international organization dedicated to advocacy, education, and research into Fluoroquinolone Toxicity. She resides in North Carolina with her husband.

Bob Brader is an award-winning actor, writer, and monologist. His acclaimed solo show, *Spitting In The Face Of The Devil*, tells the gripping, true story of discovering that his abusive ex-Marine father is a pedophile. It has won numerous awards including "Best Show" in the London Fringe. Bob has also toured internationally with his second solo show, *Preparation Hex*, a hemorrhoid tale and love story. He is currently working on his new solo show, *Smoker*. www.bobbrader.com • www.spittinginthefaceofthedevil.com

Mae L'Heureux is a twenty-something college graduate trying to find her way in the world. Passionate about diminishing the stigma surrounding mental illness, Mae speaks openly about her lived experience. Mae has recently started her career in the mental health field through nonprofit work. She loves spending time with her family and friends, traveling, reading, writing, and immersing herself in all things psychology.

Efrem Epstein is the founder of Elijah's Journey, a 501c3 focused on Suicide Awareness/Prevention in the Jewish community. He is also a member of the National Action Alliance for Suicide Prevention's Faith Communities Task Force. www.ElijahsJourney.net

Audrey Dimola always wanted to be a trapeze artist, but acrobatics of the written word have always been closest to her heart. She is the author of *Decisions We Make While We Dream*, an original collection of poetry and prose; founder of the roving reading/live writing series Nature of the Muse; and curator of the first-ever Queens Literary Town Hall, bringing together the growing literary community in her home borough. Audrey has been featured on NY1 and in the New York Daily News and has performed at venues such as Brooklyn Museum and the NYC Poetry Festival. http://audreydimola.com

Jenny Pacanowski is an Iraq veteran, writer, poet, and public speaker. She joined the Army in 2003 at age twenty-three and selected the M.O.S. of healthcare specialist/combat medic. In 2004, she was sent to Iraq. During her eleven-and-one-half-month deployment, she worked as a combat medic driving a military ambulance and serving as first-responder medical support for convoys in Iraq for the Army, Air Force, and Marines. Her poetry work has been published in Remaking Sense, After Action Review, and the Warrior Writers' Fourth Anthology. www.warriorwriters.org/Artists/jen

Jessica Gimeno is a health activist, writer, and public speaker. Her website, Fashionably Ill, is about surviving pain with style and humor. Jessica is also a contributor to The Huffington Post and Bipolar Out Loud. She has spoken at conventions for organizations like the National Alliance on Mental Illness (NAMI). Psych Central named Jessica a Mental Health Hero. MSNBC did a mental health documentary on Jessica's life. In her free time, she likes giving makeovers to women with different illnesses, spending time with her nieces and nephews, and all things New Kids on the Block. http://jessicagimeno.com

Rick Strait is a suicide attempt survivor who currently works as a therapist in Missouri as a Licensed Professional Counselor and Certified Substance Abuse Counselor. Rick's passion is working in suicide prevention and mental health awareness. He is a board member of the Eastern Chapter of Missouri AFSP and SOLOS. He provides educational trainings including Mental Health First Aid. He has helped organize multiple Suicide Awareness conferences in Missouri. Rick's unique ability to bridge his knowledge and experience provides him with a depth of understanding and practical application to better serve his clients and create effective programming.

Judy Thrasher lost her husband, Allen, to suicide in 1998 at the age of forty. She was a single mother and raised their three children following their loss. Judy has been a nurse for thirty-eight years and continues to advocate for those struggling with mental illness. Her desire is to be a beacon of hope to those who may be at the depths of despair, hopelessness, or grief. Her belief is that we must continue to live for those who have been taken from us so abruptly. Her hope is that someone may find strength in her story.

Jennifer Burton is a passionate mental health advocate and has worked in the field for ten years. She finds joy in her cherished husband, Mark, and her children Nathan, Jonathon, Jenna, and Mikayla. Her free time is spent enjoying music, writing, good books, and laughter. She resides with her family in Missouri.

Barb Smith is the founder and facilitator of the Saginaw Survivors of Suicide, which has been supporting families left behind after suicide for the past twenty-five years. Barb has received training and certifications from numerous experts in the field of suicide prevention, intervention, and the aftermath of suicide including Bill Steele, Iris Bolton, AFSP, and AAS. She has been recognized as the "Saginawian" of the year, and in 2003 she received the "Volunteer of the Year Award" from United Way.

Ashley Kowalczyk is a recent college graduate from Bradley University in Peoria, IL. While attending Bradley, Ashley was the founder and president of Bradley's Chapter of To Write Love on Her Arms for three years. After graduation, she accepted a teaching position in the Peoria Schools District and decided to stay in town. When not preparing the future of America, she enjoys Netflix, reading, and spending time with friends and family.

Jennifer Haussler Garing is a native of New Hampshire. She is a graduate of Johns Hopkins University and the University of Massachusetts Amherst. Jennifer has spoken about her experiences with suicide, mental illness, and resiliency at the American Association of Suicidology National Conference, Texas Suicide Prevention Symposium, and Austin Community College. She works as an epidemiologist in Austin, Texas where she lives in her dream home with her husband and her chocolate Lab-Rhodesian Ridgeback mix, Frannie. Jennifer is also one of the survivors profiled on livethroughthis.org.

Dana Sayre is a freelance writer living in Austin, Texas. She has a background in theatre and a MA in Performance Studies from Texas A&M University. Ms. Sayre often writes about issues of gender, sexuality, popular culture, and mental health, as well as Austin artists and events. Ms. Sayre is grateful to Josh Rivedal for this opportunity to speak on a topic about which our culture normally demands silence. In her free time, she enjoys reading, gardening, cooking, and attending or participating in performance events and festivals around Austin.

Marcia Resnick is a wife, mother, and grandmother to her grandson and grandpuppy. Professionally, she has been a math teacher and a lawyer. She is also a survivor. She has buried three of her four children, the most painful being her son who took his own life. She is active helping others who have lost a child to suicide, facilitating a support group for parents. She is also active in The American Foundation for Suicide Prevention. She skis, plays tennis, and loves the theater and traveling. She loves her family, her many friends, and life.

Kenya Casey is the Associate Director of Program Support for The Carter Center's Health Programs, providing operational support to international health programs in nine countries. Before joining The Carter Center, Kenya spent eight years at Emory University's Center for International Programs Abroad, beginning as an Advisor for students traveling to Africa and Asia and leaving as an Associate Director. For over seven years, Kenya co-facilitated dozens of diversity workshops and published manuals on recruiting underrepresented students to education abroad. Kenya obtained her B.A. in Psychology from Clark Atlanta University and her MSW from the Howard University School of Social Work.

Jamie Myre is a student leader and peer advocate with a passion for spreading empathy and understanding through her writing. She hopes to help others by sharing her experiences, whether that is with her public speaking or through writing outlets, like The i'Mpossible Project.

Ryan Cassata is a singer-songwriter and transgender motivational speaker who—all by age twenty-one—successfully cut nine records, toured the U.S., performed at some of the world's biggest Pride Festivals, won Bay Shore High School's first-ever Harvey Milk Memorial Award, became the youngest keynote speaker for the largest transgender conference in existence, appeared on TV several times, wrote two movie soundtracks, and starred in and toured with internationally screening documentary *Songs For Alexis*. www.RyanCassata.com

Matthew Shaffer is a performer, choreographer, and author of the book, *So You Want To Be A Dancer*. For more information, please visit his website, www.MatthewShaffer.com.

Claire Kaufman is a suicide prevention advocate with over seven years of planning successful suicide prevention walks. In addition, she helps those who are dealing with depression and/or suicidal thoughts through peer-to-peer programming. Claire is honored to be one of the fifty-authors in this The i'Mpossible Project book, because she wants every reader to know they aren't alone in their journey.

James Lecesne has been telling stories for over twenty-five years. His short film, *TREVOR*, won the Academy Award for Best Live Action Short and went on to inspire the founding of The Trevor Project, the only nationwide twenty-four-hour suicide prevention helpline for LGBT and Questioning youth. James is also the founder of

The After The Storm Foundation, a nonprofit organization dedicated to offering support to community centers in New Orleans that are working with youth and the arts. www.jameslecesne.com

Brent Buell is a producer, director, and novelist. He is a founding producer with Rhymes Over Beats, the hip-hop theater company bringing hip-hop to Broadway. He directed the Off-Broadway production of Josh Rivedal's comedy, *The Gospel According to Josh* (now known as *Kicking My Blue Genes in the Butt)*. For ten years, Buell volunteered with the nonprofit organization Rehabilitation Through the Arts, directing theater in New York's maximum-security prisons. His outrageous political action adventure, *Rapturous,* is available at Amazon, Barnes & Noble, or your local bookseller.

David Nathan Scott is a multi-faceted performer, on-air personality, and writer. He trained, lived, and performed for many years in New York City. He now resides in Orlando, Florida. www.davidnathanscott.com

Kenny Medrano is a consultant, social entrepreneur, hip-hop enthusiast, evolving creative, and avid backpacker. He's a New York native, raised by his mother and aunt in the great Queens County. His family is originally from Quito, Ecuador. Professionally, he started in music publishing. Years later, he became a director for a Boys & Girls Club in his childhood neighborhood. He's now the founder and chairman of Road to Greatness, Inc. whose mission is to foster leadership within individuals of all ages in order to serve, support, and expand the economic and social progress of communities.

Kathleen Myre is a freelance writer and researcher who advocates for mental health awareness and suicide prevention. By sharing her own story, she hopes to help remove the stigma associated with mental illness and inspire others to do the same. Kathleen resides with her husband and children in Nutley, New Jersey.

Nancy Tetreaux has enjoyed a twenty-plus-year HR career at major law firms, a top-four accounting/consulting firm, and large manufacturing and fashion companies, as well as nonprofits. As president of SpeakSpin, she coaches corporate leaders, managers, and small business owners in high-impact business and personal communications that include verbal, non-verbal, and written strategies. www.speakspin.com

Carlo D'Amore is an award-winning actor, playwright, and Drama Desk-nominated director with decades of experience in the theatre. Credits include Broadway, Off Broadway, regional, and international theater, as well as television and film. He has been involved in ground-breaking productions across the country. His hit solo play *No Parole*, directed by Tony Award-nominated Colman Domingo, was named one of the top ten plays in the San Francisco Bay Area and was nominated for an Audience Favorite Award at the Edinburgh Fringe Festival in Scotland.

Camilla Ross has over thirty years of theatrical experience and appeared in theatre, film, television, and radio. She has been portraying Harriet Tubman since 2009, when *Harriet Tubman's Dream* opened in collaboration with the Eugene O'Neill Theatre Center's National Theatre Institute (NTI). Camilla is president and co-founder of the Emerson Theater Collaborative and a faculty member at Three Rivers Community College. Ms. Ross is the Suicide Prevention Advocate of ETC's "I Am Worthy" project and an advocate for children and adults with Asperger's Syndrome. Camilla's latest directorial project is *Hour Father* by David H. Greer—actor, playwright, and Tony-nominated producer.

ABOUT THE CURATOR

Josh Rivedal is an author, actor, playwright, and international public speaker. He has spoken about suicide prevention, mental health awareness, and diversity in more than ninety locations across the U.S., Canada, the U.K., and Australia. He has served on the board of directors for the New York City chapter of The American Foundation for Suicide Prevention. He wrote and developed the one-man play, *Kicking My Blue Genes in The Butt* (KMBB), which has toured extensively throughout the U.S., Canada, and the U.K. His memoir *The Gospel According to Josh: A 28-Year Gentile Bar Mitzvah,* based on KMBB and published by Skookum Hill in 2013, is on The American Foundation for Suicide Prevention's recommended reading list. He writes for the Huffington Post. He is the founder and executive director of The i'Mpossible Project—a non-profit media company designed to entertain, educate, and engage on suicide prevention, mental health, diversity, and social change. Recent release in conjunction with The i'Mpossible Project: *Living Mentally Well and Crushing it While in College.* www.iampossibleproject.com

ALSO BY JOSH RIVEDAL

The Gospel According to Josh: A 28-Year Gentile Bar Mitzvah
(Based on the one-man show Kicking My Blue Genes in the Butt)

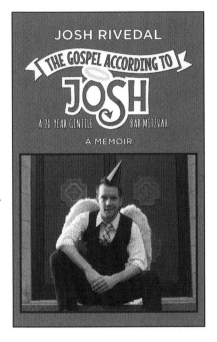

By the time Josh Rivedal turned twenty-five, he thought he'd have the perfect life—a few years singing on Broadway, followed by a starring role in his own television show. After which, his getaway home in the Hamptons would be featured in Better Homes & Gardens, and his face would grace the cover of the National Enquirer as Bigfoot's not-so-secret lover.

Instead, his resume is filled with an assortment of minor league theatre and an appearance on The Maury Povich Show—a career sidetracked by his father's suicide, a lawsuit from his mother over his inheritance, and a break-up with his long-term girlfriend. Tortured by his thoughts, he finds himself on the ledge of a fourth-floor window, contemplating jumping out to inherit his familial legacy. In turn he must reach out to the only person who can help before it's too late.

Available on Amazon, Kindle, B&N.com, and at
www.iampossibleproject.com/the-gospel-according-to-josh
On the American Foundation for Suicide Prevention's
Recommended Reading List for survivors of suicide loss

Made in the USA
Charleston, SC
02 September 2016